YORK NOTES

Hard Times

Charles Dickens

Notes by Dominic Hyland

Longman   York Press

YORK PRESS
322 Old Brompton Road, London SW5 9JH

Pearson Education Limited
Edinburgh Gate, Harlow,
Essex CM20 2JE, United Kingdom
Associated companies, branches and representatives throughout the world

First published 1997
Fourth impression 2001

ISBN 0-582-31341-4

Designed by Vicki Pacey, Trojan Horse
Illustrated by Adam Stower
Panorama of Coketown by Neil Gower
Typeset by Pantek Arts, Maidstone, Kent
Phototypeset by Gem Graphics, Trenance, Mawgan Porth, Cornwall
Colour reproduction and film output by Spectrum Colour
Produced by Pearson Education North Asia Limited, Hong Kong

Contents

PREFACE

York Notes are designed to give you a broader perspective on works of literature studied at GCSE and equivalent levels. We have carried out extensive research into the needs of the modern literature student prior to publishing this new edition. Our research showed that no existing series fully met students' requirements. Rather than present a single authoritative approach, we have provided alternative viewpoints, empowering students to reach their own interpretations of the text. York Notes provide a close examination of the work and include biographical and historical background, summaries, glossaries, analyses of characters, themes, structure and language, cultural connections and literary terms.

If you look at the Contents page you will see the structure for the series. However, there's no need to read from the beginning to the end as you would with a novel, play, poem or short story. Use the Notes in the way that suits you. Our aim is to help you with your understanding of the work, not to dictate how you should learn.

York Notes are written by English teachers and examiners, with an expert knowledge of the subject. They show you how to succeed in coursework and examination assignments, guiding you through the text and offering practical advice. Questions and comments will extend, test and reinforce your knowledge. Attractive colour design and illustrations improve clarity and understanding, making these Notes easy to use and handy for quick reference.

York Notes are ideal for:

- Essay writing
- Exam preparation
- Class discussion

The author of these Notes is Dominic Hyland. Educated at St John's College, Cambridge, and at the Universities of Manchester and Lancaster, he currently lectures in English at Blackpool and the Fylde College. He has a variety of examining experience and has written various study-aids and English textbooks.

The text used in these notes is the Penguin Classics edition, edited by Kate Flint (1995).

Hard Times was first published in 1854.

PART ONE

INTRODUCTION

HOW TO STUDY A NOVEL

You have brought this book because you wanted to study a novel on your own. This may supplement classwork.

- You will need to read the novel several times. Start by reading it quickly for pleasure, then read it slowly and carefully. Further readings will generate new ideas and help you to memorise the details of the story.

- Make careful notes on the themes, plot and characters of the novel. The plot will change some of the characters. Who changes?

- The novel may not present events chronologically. Does the novel you are reading begin at the beginning of the story or does it contain flashbacks and a muddled time sequence? Can you think why?

- How is the story told? Is it narrated by one of the characters or by an all-seeing ('omniscient') narrator?

- Does the same person tell the story all the way through? Or do we see the events through the minds and feelings of a number of different people?

- Which characters do you like or dislike? Do your sympathies change during the course of the book? Why? When?

- Any piece of writing (including your notes and essay) is the result of thousands of choices. No book had to be written in just one way: could the author of *Hard Times* have written the story differently? If events were recounted by a minor character how would this change the novel?

Studying on your own requires self-discipline and a carefully thought-out work plan in order to be effective. Good luck.

Early years

Though *Hard Times* is set in the north of England, Dickens's life is firmly lodged in the south. He was born at Portsea near Portsmouth on 7 February 1812, and christened Charles John Huffam Dickens.

Dickens's family were frequently on the move.

Two years or so later the family moved to London, to the St Pancras area.

Dickens's father was a clerk, first at the Naval Office in Portsmouth, and then in Somerset House in London. However, his father's money troubles were to be a constant reason for their moving around. He was frequently in debt despite a fairly comfortable income for that time and was, in fact, twice arrested and sent to the Marshalsea prison for debtors. Charles was spared the humiliation of lodging with the father in prison (as was the custom for families at the time), and went to stay with a Mrs Poylance, when he was just twelve. That year, too, he started work – in a blacking factory near Charing Cross, where his task was tying up and putting labels on bottles.

He did not have to stay there too long, for his father was released from prison in the same year, though his mother was not too anxious for him to leave his employment since he was earning money!

Dickens knew poverty from an early age.

Instead, Charles seemed to gain a little more security by being placed in a school in Hampstead Road, London, called Wellington House Academy. But even this was shortlived for the family was soon on the move again to a house in Somers Town where, two years later, they were evicted for not paying the rent.

At this time, though, Dickens managed to obtain a post as a solicitor's clerk. His close knowledge of the law that figures in many of his novels can be traced to this early experience.

y

Later, this was reinforced by his work as a court journalist for *The Morning Herald*, after which he spent time in Parliament when, in 1831, he worked for an uncle, John Henry Barrow, reporting for *The Mirror of Parliament*. The following year he worked for an evening paper called *The True Sun*.

Dickens's writing career

In 1833 he began broadening his scope by offering a variety of freelance articles to a number of periodicals, and three years later he collected these together and published them in book form as *Sketches by Boz*. In that same year, he produced a work about a character known

Dickens's training as a journalist helped when he came to write his novels.

as Mr Pickwick, published in monthly parts. It was so successful that he gave up his work as a journalist to write full time.

He continued to produce great novels for the next thirty years or so and *Hard Times* appeared when he was a fully established writer in 1854.

In all fifteen novels were produced at great speed. Between 1838 and 1841 for example, he wrote one novel a year.

Travel and publishing

Dickens was expanding his travels, too. He made trips to America, entertaining the Americans with readings from his novels. On a less ambitious level, he travelled to Preston in Lancashire to witness at first hand the union disputes raging there.

Concurrently with his writing, Dickens owned two literary magazines: *Household Words* and *All the Year Round*, and used them to publish his novels in serialised form. *Hard Times*, for example, was serialised in weekly parts with two chapters a week.

The work proved too much for him, finally, as did his private life to some degree. He was married for twenty-two years to Catherine Hogarth and they had thirteen children. But he met Ellen Terry, a famous actress, and lived with her. After that, he produced just three novels.

He died at the age of fifty-eight on 9 June 1870.

MEN AND MACHINES

*Troubled
times*

In the year in which Dickens was born there were riots in England. Workers felt their jobs were threatened by the widening introduction of machinery. Groups of unemployed men set about destroying machines and in that way created havoc and chaos. The movement was called the Luddite movement.

As the century progressed things gradually became worse. In 1819 there was a riot in Manchester caused by people protesting against new laws relating to the cost of food. A protest rally, in St Peter's Field there, resulted in what came to be known as the Peterloo Massacre, in which eleven people died.

*Poverty and
squalor*

*In Victorian
times, there was
an alarming
contrast between
rich and poor.*

While the owners of the industries were prosperous – Mr Bounderby in *Hard Times* is a classic example – the workers were poorly fed and poorly housed. Their working conditions, whether in factories or mines, were appalling. Even women or children could be expected to work up to fifteen hours a day, for six days a week. The monotony and horror of it is found in Chapter 5, 'The Key-note', in *Hard Times*. Coketown 'had a black canal in it, and a river that ran purple with ill-smelling dye, and vast piles of buildings full of windows where there was always a rattling and a trembling all day long'. It was 'inhabited with people ... who all went in and out at the same hours ... to do the same work, and to whom every day was the same as yesterday and tomorrow'.

*Thomas
Carlyle*

Dickens dedicated *Hard Times* to a philosopher friend of his, Thomas Carlyle, who felt very strongly that society was threatened by the industrialisation of England. In 1829 he made the following statement in a work he called 'Signs of the Times': 'It is the age of machinery in every outward and inward sense of that word. Nothing is now done directly or by hand; all is by rule and calculated contrivance .... Men are grown mechanical in head and in heart, as well as in hand'.

Throughout *Hard Times* Dickens refers to the workers as 'Hands', men and women who are only important to their masters because they can manage machines. Dickens says they have lost any sense of the importance and value of the individual:

> So many hundred Hands in this Mill; so many hundred horse Steam Power. It is known, to the force of a single pound weight, what the engine will do; but not all the calculation of the National Debt can tell me the capacity for good or evil, for love or hatred, for patriotism or discontent, for the decomposition of virtue or vice, or the reverse, at any single moment in the soul of one of these quiet servants, with the composed faces and the regulated actions (Chapter 11).

Trade unions

In 1854 when *Hard Times* was written, trade unions had only been legal for thirty years. There was still a strong bias against the workers in the laws governing them. Mass union action was largely impossible, and organised trade unions belonged to skilled trades only.

Dickens's description of Coketown was based on eye-witness reporting.

To gain first-hand knowledge of union activities amongst the cotton workers of Preston (the 'Coketown' of *Hard Times*) Dickens travelled to the Lancashire town. There had been a strike there lasting several weeks. A ballad that was circulating at that time described the event:

... The working people such as we
Pass their time in misery
While they live in luxury
The Cotton Lords of Preston.
They're making money every way
And building factories every day

Yet when we ask them for more pay
They had the impudence to say:
'To your demands we'll not consent
You get enough, so be content.'
But we will have our ten per cent
From the Cotton Lords of Preston.

Dickens's
description of
a trade union
meeting was
not entirely
favourable.

Thomas Carlyle was not one really to encourage trade unions. Dickens, too, was not obviously in favour of organised labour. We are not encouraged to admire Slackbridge, the trade union orator. We read in the 'Men and Brothers' chapter: 'He was not so honest, he was not so manly, he was not so good-humoured; he substituted cunning for their simplicity, and passion for their safe solid sense. An ill-made, high-shouldered man, with lowering brows, and his features crushed into an habitually stern expression, he contrasted most unfavourably, even in his mongrel dress, with the great body of his hearers in their plain working clothes.'

The negative impression we have of him in this description is reinforced by his unfair treatment of Stephen Blackpool. His fellow trade unionists, too, are depicted as less than admirable in their harsh attitude to Stephen: 'By general consent, they even avoided that side of the street on which he habitually walked.'

Town life

Dickens attacks the town environment in the novel just as he does in many other of his works. The classic portrayal of Coketown which we find in 'The Key-note' chapter is reinforced later in 'Stephen Blackpool' where Dickens presents us with a vivid picture: 'Nature was as strongly bricked out as the killing airs and gases were bricked in; at the heart of the labyrinth of narrow courts upon courts, and close streets upon streets … and the whole an unnatural family, shouldering, and trampling, and pressing one another to death.'

People lived in back-to-back houses, lacking ventilation and indoor sanitation.

y

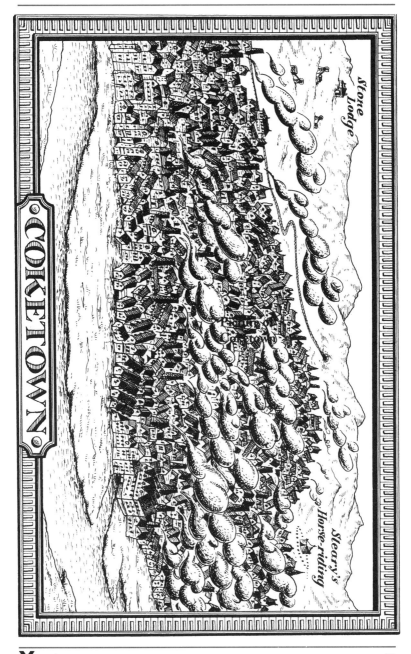

A contemporary of Dickens, Elizabeth Gaskell, offers
this description of Manchester in the 1850s:

Note how similar   … the streets, uneven, fallen into ruts, and in parts

in feeling this   without drains or pavement; masses of refuse, offal,

description is to   and sickening filth lie among standing pools in all

those of poverty in   directions; the atmosphere is poisoned by the effluvia

Coketown.   from these, and laden and darkened by the smoke of
a dozen tall factory chimneys …. The race that lived
in these ruinous cottages, behind broken windows,
mended with oil-skins, spring doors, and rotten door
posts, or in dark, wet cellars, in measureless filth and
stench, in this atmosphere penned in as if with a
purpose, this race must really have reached the lowest
stage of humanity.

PART TWO

SUMMARIES

GENERAL SUMMARY

Book the First: The novel opens in the classroom, where Thomas
Sowing Gradgrind is addressing the class in what is called his
'model school'. He is insisting on the value of facts and
the dangers of the imagination. It is ironic (see Literary
Terms) that immediately after this he finds his two
eldest children, Tom and Louisa, seeking the very thing
he was denouncing: the expression of the imagination.
They are peeping into a circus ring. Further irony is
added by the fact that Gradgrind had earlier rebuked a
child called Sissy Jupe whose father works at the circus.
It would at this point be more accurate to say that
Sissy's father had worked at the circus, for he has
recently abandoned it and his daughter.

It had been Gradgrind's intention to advise Mr Jupe
(or, as he is known at the circus, Signor Jupe) that his
daughter could no longer attend the school. Instead,
despite the harsh impression we have of Gradgrind, he
agrees to accept the now abandoned Sissy into his own
household as a companion to his daughter Louisa. He
is warned of the ill consequences of this action by his
friend Josiah Bounderby – a rich industrialist who, we
learn, has always been inordinately fond of Louisa.
Indeed, later in this first Book, Bounderby makes clear
his desire to marry Louisa. Louisa, on her part, agrees
to the marriage simply to please her brother, Tom, who
is looking for a position in Bounderby's bank. Louisa is
eighteen and Bounderby fifty when they marry.

Shortly before his marriage to Louisa, Bounderby agrees
to an interview with a worker at his mill named Stephen
Blackpool, who is much troubled by his unhappy
marriage. He has been married for nineteen years but the

13

marriage has not been a success. His wife is an alcoholic and has been unfaithful to him. He asks Bounderby for advice on how to gain release from his wife. Bounderby and his housekeeper, Mrs Sparsit, are appalled by the suggestion of divorce and can offer Stephen no help or consolation. He is in love with another woman called Rachael and is anxious to marry her.

Soon after this we meet Rachael. She is nursing Stephen's sick wife who has returned unannounced to Stephen's impoverished lodgings. On his way back to these lodgings Stephen had met an old woman who, we later find, is called Mrs Pegler, and is Bounderby's much abused mother. After Bounderby's marriage Mrs Sparsit takes up residence over Bounderby's bank whilst Louisa and Bounderby take a house in the country.

Book the Second: Reaping

In the country Louisa and Mr Bounderby are visited by James Harthouse, an idle gentleman of good family who is vaguely interested in 'going in' for politics.

The story rapidly changes from a study of industrial life – though there is a vital section dealing with industrial relations – into a kind of detective story. For Tom robs the bank and implicates the unfortunate Stephen Blackpool, who has been befriended by his sister Louisa. As luck would have it, the robbery coincides with Stephen's departure from Coketown after he had been rejected by his work-mates for disobeying trade union rules. This strand of the plot runs parallel with another, dealing with the apparently illicit relationship between Louisa and James Harthouse, which is being spied on by the vengeful Mrs Sparsit.

Book the Third: Garnering

Louisa, disturbed by Harthouse's advances, leaves Bounderby and returns to her father's.

Bounderby offers a reward for Blackpool's arrest, and Rachael traces him and begs him to come home. But on the way, Stephen falls down a disused mine shaft, and, after being rescued, dies.

The chase now turns into the pursuit of the real criminal, Tom, who is helped by Sissy Jupe, to make his escape through Sleary's circus and board ship for America, never to return.

DETAILED SUMMARIES

BOOK THE FIRST: SOWING

CHAPTER 1
The one thing needful

Gradgrind is not yet identified by name.

The novel opens with the booming voice of Mr Gradgrind filling a large classroom with his sentiments about 'Facts', and the need for a pragmatic (or practical) view of the world. This, for him, is the essence of a sound education. His appearance is threatening and unattractive. He is accompanied by two other adults, one a schoolmaster, the other anonymous.

COMMENT

Book titles – Sowing, Reaping, Garnering – have a biblical ring. In the New Testament Christ makes a lot of references in his messages to the world to ideas related to farming as a kind of parallel to finding our way to heaven. One of his best known statements was: 'As ye sow, so shall ye reap'. In plainer English it simply means that the outcome of an event will depend on what we originally put into it.

Here the three terms are to be seen as referring to the upbringing and education of the children. Whatever happens in childhood will have a direct bearing on what happens when they grow up.

Note Dickens's chapter heading, 'The One Thing Needful', a biblical reference.

Dickens's fondness for character description is shown here in his vivid depiction of an anonymous male character with a bald head on which what hair he had was like 'a plantation of firs to keep the wind off its shining surface'.

GLOSSARY
commodious cellarage eye-sockets which resemble deep cellars
skirts of his bald head the fringe of hair around his bald head
obstinate carriage his stubborn and unmoving stance
little vessels Dickens compares the heads of the young children to empty containers which are to be filled
imperial gallons the standard measure of liquids (4.54 litres)

CHAPTER 2

Murdering the Innocents

Note the title's biblical reference to Herod's slaughtering of male infants.

Thomas Gradgrind, the speaker, is now described in greater detail. He addresses one of the pupils, identifying her by number in the class and not by her name. She introduces herself as Sissy Jupe. He takes offence at this version of her given name and insists that she call herself Cecilia. When she points out that her father calls her Sissy he questions her about her father, who works with horses in a circus. Gradgrind then insists on hearing a definition of a horse, and when Sissy fails to produce it, another pupil called Bitzer promptly delivers a dictionary definition of one.

Though a minor character, Bitzer will appear throughout the novel.

At this point, one of the other adults in the room – obviously an inspector of schools – asks his own question of the class: would they paper a room in their house with pictures of horses. The children's first response is in the affirmative. His obvious disapproval persuades them to change this to the negative! The only dissenters are a fat boy and Sissy Jupe. The first is soon dealt with, but Sissy proves to be much less amenable. She puts the case for the play of the imagination but is promptly shouted down by the inspector. He then yields place to the probation teacher, M'Choakumchild. Dickens describes the type of training this teacher received and suggests that it was inappropriate to what should have been his goals in education.

COMMENT   Bitzer is a minor character in the story but note how
often he appears throughout. Sissy is much more
significant and is there to exemplify the way in which
imagination is preferable, in Dickens's eyes, to mere
facts. She knows what a horse is since she has worked
with them. Bitzer can only give a cold definition.

Dickens's tendency to exaggeration and repetition is
well exemplified here, as well as his fondness for names
that seem to sum up the character. M'Choakumchild is
a classic example of this.

GLOSSARY   little pitchers another reference to the 'vessels' in Chapter 1
waiting to be filled with facts
girl number twenty in large classrooms at the time there were so
many pupils that they were given numbers for ease of
reference

CHAPTER 3

A loophole

Thomas Gradgrind makes his way home to Stone
Lodge and Dickens once more enlarges on the need, as
Gradgrind sees it, for a factual approach to life. We
learn that there are five children in the Gradgrind
family. They have all been reared on the principle of
fact and the avoidance of wonder. They had never, for
example, heard any nursery rhymes or fairy stories.

Bounderby is a larger than life figure.

With this as a background it is easy to imagine Gradgrind's annoyance when on his way home he finds two of his children, Louisa and Tom, stealing a peep at the circus which has come to town and in which Sissy Jupe's father is a star performer. When confronted by her father Louisa defends herself bravely and expresses her disillusionment with life. She is, as Dickens tells us, 'fifteen or sixteen'. Gradgrind insists that the two children should go home with him and, as they go along, his total concern appears to be what Mr Bounderby would think of them if he ever discovered their misdeed.

COMMENT The Gradgrind children already show signs of rebellion – a feature that will be in evidence in their adult life. Tom is to rob a bank and Louisa is to contemplate adultery with James Harthouse.

The close bond between Louisa and her brother, Tom, will be exploited by Tom in adult life.

The construction of the story caused Dickens a lot of concern. He wrote to a friend: 'I am in a dreary state planning and planning the story of *Hard Times*'. He uses links between the three households of the Jupes, Gradgrinds and Bounderby to help add a sense of unity in the novel.

Humour is rare in this serious novel. The episode with Merrylegs and Signor Jupe does offer some light relief.

GLOSSARY **a face in the moon** the face banished to the moon for gathering sticks on the Sabbath (traditional nursery tale)

Professor Owen Sir Richard Owen (1804–92), a physician and comparative anatomist, not a star-gazer as Dickens's humour might suggest

Charles's Wain another star formation

that famous cow reference to nursery rhyme 'The House that Jack Built'

Tom Thumb the main character in a fairy story of that name
conchological to do with shells
Peter Piper reference to children's tongue-twister
in an ecclesiastical niche of early Gothic architecture humorous
reference to Sleary's 'box office', which is compared to a
recess in a medieval church housing a saint's statue
House of Correction prison where convicts underwent
reformatory treatment under very harsh conditions
Mrs Grundy prudish old lady, much feared by her neighbours,
from the play *Speed the Plough*

CHAPTER 4

Mr Bounderby

*Notice how Mrs
Gradgrind is
totally feeble and
submissive.*

An immediate link between the conclusion of the last chapter and the beginning of this one is made. Where Gradgrind could be summed up as square, Bounderby, by contrast, is round like a balloon. He, like Gradgrind, is bald. We first meet him standing in front of the fire at Stone Lodge talking to Mrs Gradgrind of the poverty he experienced in his youth, and how he overcame that poverty to become a successful self-made man. Mrs Gradgrind is plagued by ill-health. As a mother she is as useless as the mother who, Bounderby claims, abandoned him as a child. When Thomas Gradgrind enters the room with the two culprits, Tom and Louisa, Mrs Gradgrind can only complain that their actions have aggravated her headache.

In the conversation which follows Gradgrind and Bounderby establish to their satisfaction that Sissy Jupe's presence in the school has had a bad effect on the Gradgrind children. They agree that she must be forced to leave the school immediately, and they set off to inform her father of that fact. Before leaving, Bounderby shows his interest in Louisa by giving her a kiss and calling her 'my pet'.

COMMENT

Caricature (see Literary Terms) is one way in which some humour is added to the novel. It consists mainly of exaggerating a physical feature, and in Bounderby's case it is his roundness.

We are introduced to three other Gradgrinds and Dickens has chosen very apt names for two of them. Adam Smith and Malthus are historical figures associated with industrialisation and population growth.

Notice how Jane Gradgrind falls asleep over her sums. It is a nice, poignant effect.

Bounderby's interest in Louisa, and her growing hardness of nature, are two key points. She is becoming indifferent about her fate. Here her concluding words to Tom show how strong her indifference is: 'You may cut the piece out with your penknife, if you like, Tom. I wouldn't cry'.

GLOSSARY   chandler a dealer in candles and groceries
Adam Smith Scottish economist (1723–90) who advocated free trade and *laissez-faire*
Thomas Robert Malthus English economist and churchman (1766–1834) who advocated population control

CHAPTER 5

The key-note
Note the appalling
description of
Coketown.

Dickens describes Coketown in all its horror. He makes an attack on the soulless architecture of the place as well as the irrelevance of the spiritual features of the town. He draws an analogy between the soullessness of Coketown and the bleak rationalism of the Gradgrinds.

Gradgrind and Bounderby are searching for Signor Jupe and have been told that he lives at Pod's End. They are suddenly halted by the sight of Sissy Jupe pursued by Bitzer who literally bumps into Gradgrind. The latter rebukes him and sends him on his way. Gradgrind then asks Sissy to take them to her father, to which she readily agrees.

y

COMMENT

This chapter's most significant feature is the description of Coketown, which it is interesting to compare with the opening of Dickens's novel *Bleak House*.

Dickens describes a chapel as 'a pious warehouse of red brick' with 'a bell in a bird-cage' on top.

Religion is another focus of Dickens's attack in this novel, and this is coupled with a similar attack here on the 'Teetotal Society'. Dickens was always suspicious of such so-called charities. It's interesting to find that his friend Carlyle, referred to earlier in these Notes, wrote about religion along similar lines. He says religious organisations appear to have high ideals but are sometimes more interested in less admirable things. In his 'Signs of the Times' Carlyle writes:

> Then, we have Religious machines, of all imaginable varieties; the Bible society, professing a far higher and heavenly structure, is found, on enquiry, to be an altogether earthly contrivance: supported by collection of moneys, by fomenting of vanities, by puffing, intrigue and chicane; a machine for converting the heathen.

Note the pursuit of Sissy by Bitzer. We shall find him in pursuit of others in the novel, all in the interests of what he sees as good.

GLOSSARY

Teetotal Society a reference to the many temperance societies flourishing during this time whose members refrained from alcohol

Mocha coffee fine coffee, originally from Mocha, an Arabian port

CHAPTER 6

Sleary's horsemanship

Sissy takes Gradgrind and Bounderby to the Pegasus's Arms where she and her father live. She expects to find him there together with his dog, Merrylegs. But they are not there, and she leaves Gradgrind and Bounderby at the inn while she goes in search of her father. While she is away, a couple of performers from the circus, E.W.B. Childers and a dwarf known as Kidderminster, inform the two men that Sissy's father has left for good,

Y

abandoning his daughter. Childers points out that he probably did so, ironically (see Literary Terms), in his daughter's best interests, and he tells Gradgrind and Bounderby that Signor Jupe was particularly concerned that she should receive proper schooling.

Note how Dickens suggests an exotic lifestyle with 'peacock's feathers and a pigtail bolt upright' hanging on a nail.

At this juncture, all the circus folk appear, including their leader, Sleary. He asks the visitors to be kind to Sissy when she comes back. But Bounderby, intent on facts, tells Sissy bluntly that her father has left her. The circus performers are annoyed at his lack of feeling, and Sleary hints that they might throw Bounderby out of the window. Gradgrind saves the day by assuring Sissy that she may stay at the school and live in his house if she so wishes. If she decides to stay with him, though, she must on no account have any dealings with the circus people. Sleary, on his part, assures Sissy that she would be welcome to stay with them. Sissy is assured that her father could always find her at Gradgrind's. She collects her belongings, having decided on Gradgrind and on education.

COMMENT

At the end of the last chapter, Gradgrind was given a more positive portrayal: 'His character was not unkind … it might have been a very kind one indeed, if he had only made some round mistake in the arithmetic that balanced it, years ago'. Here, his kindness is shown dramatically in his offering Sissy Jupe a home, now that her father has left her.

There is a real degree of sadness, here, created by Dickens's portrayal of the kind circus people, Sissy Jupe's loss, and even the speech impediment given to Sleary.

GLOSSARY

Pegasus a winged horse (Greek mythology)
a pigtail bolt upright the comical cap used by Jupe in his circus act
Centaur half-man, half-horse (Greek mythology)
carmine a crimson pigment made from cochineal, applied here to the face for redness

Cupid Roman god of love
goosed hissed and booed by an audience
Dick Jones of Wapping a person of no importance
Punch comic figure in a puppet play
morrithed 'morrised' or 'run away'. The term comes from the
morris dance – a quick skipping folk dance (Sleary
mispronounces 's' as 'th')

CHAPTER 7

Mrs Sparsit

Mrs Sparsit, a character of eccentric appearance, with an odd background, claims to come from a respectable family but has fallen on hard times. She is now housekeeper to Bounderby, who treats her with great respect. Having a housekeeper adds, of course, to his self-esteem.

Sissy Jupe is at this time staying at Bounderby's before going to Stone Lodge. Bounderby has insisted on this to give Gradgrind time to reflect on his decision to give Sissy a home. Bounderby is not sympathetic to Sissy and is concerned that she might in some way contaminate Louisa. Mrs Sparsit tries to ingratiate herself with Bounderby by saying: 'You are quite another father to Louisa, sir'. Bounderby insists, however, that he is better seen as a father to Tom Gradgrind whom he plans to employ at the bank once Tom has finished his education. This conversation with Mrs Sparsit is interrupted by the arrival of Gradgrind and Louisa who have come to collect Sissy. The three of them set off for Stone Lodge without exchanging a word.

COMMENT

Look for the ways in which Dickens holds the novel together. Apparently minor characters, like Mrs Sparsit and Sissy Jupe, are used to help link people and events.

Minor characters are used to link the novel together.

Gradgrind continues to impress by his kindness to Sissy, and this is in contrast to Bounderby's unnatural interest in Louisa.

GLOSSARY

horse flesh, blind hookey a typically Dickensian list of random associations calculated to indicate chaos in business affairs

blind hookey a card game
a mysterious leg humorous way of saying that the old lady had
been bedridden for a long time
Coriolanian adjective from Coriolanus, depicted by Shakespeare
as fierce and aggressive
Magna Charta Magna Carta, the agreement signed by King John
of England in 1215 guaranteeing certain rights to his subjects
Habeas Corpus legal provision requiring that a person held in
custody be presented to a judge by a certain time for a
decision as to the legality of his imprisonment
Bill of Rights statute passed in England in 1689 after the
deposing of King James II
Princes and Lords the two lines quoted here are from Oliver
Goldsmith's (1730–74) famous poem The Deserted Village
the tumbling girl a reference to Sissy and the circus where she
would have performed acrobatics

CHAPTER 8

Never wonder

Louisa shows real
affection for her
brother.

Dickens once again recapitulates the theme of fact
versus fancy and repeats that in Coketown those in
charge of education will only accept facts. The
populace, though, he points out, naturally seek to
escape from the drudgery of a fact. His key examples
of the product of a factual education, Tom and Louisa,
are found in conversation. Tom is bewailing his life and
remarking that Sissy Jupe is being treated in the same
stultifying manner as he and Louisa. Unlike everyone
else, he is able to get Louisa to show some emotion,
and he exhibits an understanding of Bounderby's
designs on her. He tells Louisa that he plans to use this
to his own advantage in gaining employment at
Bounderby's bank, which he regards as a means of
escape from his home. The chapter ends, as it began,
with reflections on the use of the imagination. Louisa
is confessing to Tom that she finds some delight in
letting her imagination roam. Whilst she is speaking,
Mrs Gradgrind enters and expresses concern that after
such a scientific education her children should still
wish to wonder.

COMMENT   There is some inconsistency here in the portrayal of
Louisa, who once again returns to a fondness for the
world of the imagination.

There is also a sudden development in the plot in Tom's
express intention of acquiring employment in the bank
and using Louisa's influence to help his scheme.

GLOSSARY   **De Foe** Daniel Defoe (1660–1731), English author best known
for his novels *Robinson Crusoe* and *Moll Flanders*
Euclid Greek mathematician most noted for his use of logic
Cocker Edward Cocker (1631–75), English engraver and
schoolmaster known for his copy-book of writing exercises and
his *Cocker's Arithmetic*. The phrase 'according to Cocker'
came to mean 'absolutely correct'

CHAPTER 9   There is an irony (see Literary Terms) in the chapter
title, for in terms of the Gradgrind philosophy, Sissy is
Sissy's progress   not making progress at all. She is caught, as Dickens
says, between M'Choakumchild and Mrs Gradgrind.
The only thing that keeps her with the Gradgrinds is
her firm belief that her father will one day return. She
tells Louisa of the real love that exists between her and
her father. The conversation is interrupted by Tom who
urges Louisa to join her father and Bounderby in the
drawing-room. He hopes that Louisa will help him
curry favour with Bounderby.

COMMENT   No real advances are made to the plot here, except to
say that Tom's plans are already in motion.

Some further evidence of the maturing of Louisa's
character is provided in her wish to share an emotional
life.

GLOSSARY   **whether the Sultan** reference to the stories of Scheherazade,
who in the *Arabian Nights* marries the Sultan and saves her
life by entertaining him night after night with her tales

CHAPTER 10

Stephen Blackpool

Stephen is not a very attractive person though we are meant to sympathise with him.

We are introduced to a new character, Stephen Blackpool. He is one of those thousands of workers who live in Coketown. Though only forty years old he is, as Dickens says, already an old man. He is seen waiting outside the works for his friend, Rachael, a woman of thirty-five; he likes to walk her home despite the gossiping neighbours, after which he makes his way to his own lodgings. When he arrives there, he is surprised by the presence of a woman – 'a disabled, drunken creature'. They obviously know one another though at this point Dickens does not tell us who she is.

COMMENT   It may be that Dickens felt the need to give his novel added interest. He does so by introducing the sub-plot of the relationship between Stephen and Rachael.

The novel deals with injustice and industrialisation throughout, but, so far perhaps, only in a general manner. Now, with the focus on Stephen Blackpool we have a very particular instance of someone who experiences both at first hand!

The final part of the chapter shows Dickens's fondness for surprise and mystery at work. It is something of a cliff-hanger: 'Who is this drunken woman?' He will make us wait to find out.

CHAPTER 11

No way out

Stephen seeks an interview with Bounderby, his employer, to ask advice on the question of marriage and divorce, for that drunken woman of the last chapter is Stephen's wife. Owing to the strict conditions of his employment Stephen must use his lunch break to see Bounderby, and Dickens contrasts 'the little bread' that Stephen had for his lunch with the sumptuous meal being enjoyed by his employer. Mrs Sparsit (introduced in Chapter 7), is still Bounderby's housekeeper; she

witnesses not only his meal, though, but his decisions,
too. Indeed, she contributes to the sense of moral
outrage expressed by Bounderby on hearing of
Stephen's wish to be divorced. She and Bounderby
make it clear to Stephen that there is, as the chapter
heading suggests, no way out of his situation.

COMMENT   It's worth remembering that though the answer to the
mystery posed at the end of the previous chapter comes
quickly for us, Victorian readers had to wait for the
next weekly edition of *Household Words* to appear before
they found out!

Industrial conditions come in for more violent criticism
here with Dickens's use of the imagery (see Literary
Terms) of elephants and serpents. It stands in sharp
contrast to the luxury enjoyed by Bounderby.

Bounderby's moral indignation has to be seen as sheer
hypocrisy in the light of his cruel exploitation of his
workers.

GLOSSARY   Eas'r Monday nineteen year sin Easter Monday nineteen years ago
played old Gooseberry created chaos
brigg bridge
Doctors' Commons a law court in London at which Dickens was
once a reporter

CHAPTER 12

The old   Having left Bounderby, Stephen encounters an old
woman   woman who asks him who lives in the house which he
has just left. She establishes that it is Bounderby and she
asks about his health and appearance. She has come, she
tells Stephen, that very day after a long journey – a
journey which she makes every year just to catch a
glimpse of Bounderby. She seems to have no other
interest than that, and certainly makes much of Stephen
when she finds that he works at Bounderby's mill.

y

COMMENT   We had been held in suspense about the identity of one
           woman and now Dickens uses the same technique,
           inviting the reader to join in another guessing game.
           Who is this old woman? Why is she so interested in
           Bounderby? We are invited to read on!

GLOSSARY   **Hummobee** a humming bee
           Parliamentary a train on which fares were cheaper than normal
           patricians foremost citizens
           Divine Right a reference to the notion that men's affairs are
           directly ordered by God
           Towers of Babel a reference to the story in the Old Testament in
           which men sought to defy the Almighty by building their way to
           heaven. God punished them by causing confusion in communication

CHAPTER 13

Rachael

Rachael is an angelic sort of woman.

Stephen eventually forces himself to go home. There he
sees a candle burning in the window and finds Rachael
in his room. She is tending his wife, who is desperately
ill. Rachael tells him that she must stay to look after his
wife as long as she can. She also persuades Stephen to
sleep for a while.

In his sleep Stephen has a terrifying dream in which his
wedding day turns into the day of his execution on the
gallows. Then, between sleep and waking, he senses that
his wife is awake and is stretching her hand towards a
bottle of poison near the bed. Stephen in his present
condition is unable to do anything but at the crucial
moment Rachael intervenes and prevents suicide. The
chapter concludes with Rachael's departure leaving
Stephen in charge of his sick wife.

COMMENT   Dickens relies a great deal on exaggeration here. If a
           character is evil, he or she may have no appealing feature;
           if the character is good, he or she may have no faults at
           all. This is another way of painting a caricature (see
           Literary Terms). Rachael is an appropriate example of
           someone who epitomises (see Literary Terms) goodness.

y

Dickens enjoys a great sense of drama, and there is plenty of evidence of this here. We have the fitful dream that Stephen has and the sensational account of the rescue of Stephen's wife by Rachael. Dickens invites the reader to say: 'If only Rachael had been less good, poor Stephen's life would have been so much happier'.

CHAPTER 14

The great manufacturer

Note Dickens's use of suspense.

We are re-introduced to some of the leading figures in Dickens's main plot, namely, the Gradgrinds and Sissy Jupe. Some time has passed and Louisa is now a woman. Sissy has completed her education, and Tom Gradgrind is working for Bounderby. Thomas Gradgrind has been elected to Parliament. Dickens introduces yet another touch of mystery by keeping Louisa – as well as his readers – waiting for some time for a crucial discussion with her father. But the subject of this discussion is anticipated by Tom who tells her that Bounderby is involved in some plan with their father. The fact that Mrs Sparsit is not in Bounderby's confidence in this matter offers us a further hint that what he has to say to Gradgrind will involve Louisa.

COMMENT

Dickens has used the Stephen Blackpool episodes to help suggest the passing of time. However, it may seem a little unconvincing that so much appears to have happened to the other characters, in what seems really a short time.

There is a further hint of mystery here: why does Bounderby want an interview with Gradgrind?

There are, however, features we recognise in three of the major characters: Tom Gradgrind is still scheming, Louisa still sees images in the fire, and Sissy Jupe, poignantly, still keeps the bottle of oil for soothing her father's feet, should he ever return home.

CHAPTER 15

Father and   In an interview the following morning Thomas
daughter   Gradgrind acquaints Louisa of Bounderby's proposal of
                      marriage. Louisa proves quite difficult and embarrasses
Louisa's marriage   her father by the nature of her questions: will Bounderby
to Bounderby is to expect her to love him for example? It is made clear that
be one of   Bounderby only wishes to marry her – there is no
convenience.   immediate demand that she love him! Louisa agrees on
                      these practical terms of marriage, and the news is
                      communicated to Mrs Gradgrind. Sissy is there at the
                      time, and Dickens tells us that from that time the
                      relationship between her and Louisa changes for the
                      worse: Louisa becomes 'impassive, proud, and cold'.

COMMENT   Earlier on we had anticipated an improvement in
                     Gradgrind's character. But here that seems to have
                     disappeared in his treatment of Louisa, who is
                     something of a pawn in the plans of Gradgrind and
                     Bounderby.

Suitability in the Louisa, too, seems resigned to live without happiness.
match depended   She accepts this marriage of convenience with
on 'means and   Bounderby, and at the end of the chapter Dickens has
positions',   some harsh things to say about her. However, he does
according to Mr   allow Louisa to express her discontent with her
Gradgrind.   upbringing, and especially the fact that she was never
                      encouraged to develop her emotions.

                      As suggested earlier, there is little humour in this novel.
                      However, a sense of madness is revealed in Gradgrind's
                      absurd use of statistics, and the portrayal of Mrs
                      Gradgrind, who seems comically obsessed with what to
                      call her future son-in-law!

GLOSSARY   Blue Beard villain, in a traditional tale, who is noted for the
                     murder of several wives
                     blue books official government reports based on statistics, so
                     called because of their blue covers

Y

Tartary the empire established by Genghis Khan in medieval
times in central Asia and eastern Europe

Calmucks a Mongolian tribe

CHAPTER 16

Husband and   The plot now moves at a fast pace. The proposal of the
wife   previous chapter becomes a reality. Bounderby marries
                 Louisa. Before doing so, he has had to overcome the
Mrs Sparsit's embarrassing situation of Mrs Sparsit. He does so
hopes are dashed. without any apparent difficulty. She readily
                 congratulates him on his engagement and, equally
                 readily, agrees to move to lodgings over the bank.
                 Agreeable terms are reached, including a private
                 apartment for her there and an annual allowance. Within
                 weeks of his proposal and Louisa's acceptance they are
                 married and leave for their honeymoon in France.

COMMENT   Mrs Sparsit dominates this chapter. She stands in sharp
                 contrast, for example, with the 'recumbent' and
                 eccentric Mrs Gradgrind. It is she, too, who is central
                 to the wedding plans. There is a real sense that Mrs
                 Sparsit had expected to be the bride, and not Louisa, in
                 her apparent good wishes to Bounderby: there is a barb,
                 'I fondly hope that Miss Gradgrind may be all you
                 desire, *and deserve*'.

                 Mrs Sparsit's ready acceptance of Bounderby's
                 commitment to Louisa may be attributable to the fact
                 that Dickens had to manage his plot very tightly. He
                 had complained to a friend when talking about *Hard
                 Times* that 'the difficulty of space is crushing'.

GLOSSARY   break the looking glass an expression of anger
                 Don't go to the North Pole Mr Bounderby's exaggerated way of
                 telling Mrs Sparsit to stay near the fire
                 bottoms a reference to ships' bottoms

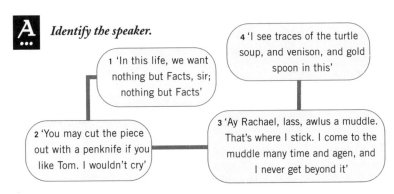

A *Identify the speaker.*

1 'In this life, we want nothing but Facts, sir; nothing but Facts'

4 'I see traces of the turtle soup, and venison, and gold spoon in this'

2 'You may cut the piece out with a penknife if you like Tom. I wouldn't cry'

3 'Ay Rachael, lass, awlus a muddle. That's where I stick. I come to the muddle many time and agen, and I never get beyond it'

Identify the person 'to whom' this comment refers.

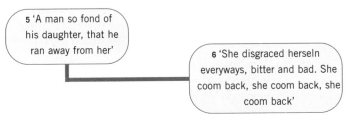

5 'A man so fond of his daughter, that he ran away from her'

6 'She disgraced herseln everyways, bitter and bad. She coom back, she coom back, she coom back'

Check your answers on page 85.

B *Consider these issues.*

a How Dickens creates immediate physical effects in characters.

b Which characters he seems to sympathise with most, and which he depicts as unattractive.

c What each of the circus people contributes to our understanding of the novel so far.

d What evidence there is so far of the reason for choosing *Hard Times* as the title to the novel.

<table>
<tr><td>CHAPTER 1

Effects in the bank</td><td>A year has passed since the wedding of Bounderby and Louisa. Mrs Sparsit now lives in chambers above the bank. One of the servants in her establishment is Bitzer, the schoolboy of the earlier 'Murdering the Innocents' chapter.</td></tr>
</table>

It is a hot summer's afternoon, and Mrs Sparsit is sitting at the window of her room looking over what Dickens calls a 'frying street'. Bitzer is shown to be her spy who reports to her, particularly on the actions of Tom and Louisa. She still looks down on Bounderby and sees him as the 'victim' of his marriage.

A stranger tells Mrs Sparsit and Bitzer that he is looking for Bounderby the banker. Dickens does not give us his name, but the description of his dress and manner, and the fact that he puts 'no more faith in anything than Lucifer' indicates that he is probably up to no good! He has been given a letter of introduction to Bounderby by Gradgrind whom he met in London.

<table>
<tr><td>COMMENT</td><td>We have another example of the intrusion of a new character for whom we have as yet no name, and who gives rise to a variety of questions needing to be answered. Why has he lost his way to the bank when he is so obviously worldly wise? Why has he an interest in Louisa? Why does he seem so intent on flattering Mrs Sparsit?</td></tr>
<tr><td>*Bounderby and fellow industrialists are singled out for attack.*</td><td>Industry is another focal point here. Dickens suggests that government efforts to improve the lot of the workers are constantly thwarted by employers who simply threaten to close their factories down.</td></tr>
</table>

Opposition to the industrialists is provided by the mention of trade union organisation. It is important to assess how far you find Dickens to be in sympathy or not with the trade union movement.

CHAPTER 2

Mr James
Harthouse

Dickens now divulges the name of the stranger and describes his meeting with Bounderby. Harthouse is a man-about-town, an idler who has tried most things and found them boring. He has been persuaded by his brother to curry favour with the 'Hard Facts' party of which Gradgrind is a member. He, it is believed, will give that party a touch of class; he will be able to 'sell' the party to sections of the public which it would not normally be able to reach. The plan has worked. He has successfully ingratiated himself with Gradgrind who now introduces him to wealth in the person of Bounderby. He would, however, have quickly tired of this, had he not also been introduced to Louisa. He finds her both attractive and a challenge to his male ego. Through Tom Gradgrind, he sees a way of reaching Louisa's affections.

COMMENT

The build-up of an attack on industrialists continues. Especially effective is Bounderby's ludicrous statement: 'First of all, you see our smoke …. It's the healthiest thing in the world in all respects, and particularly for the lungs.'

James Harthouse is a further example of a 'type'. If Bounderby is an exaggerated version of the 'self-made' man, then Harthouse stands as the stereotype (see Literary Terms) of the idle rich. He has no real purpose in life except to try out various interests, and he is easily bored.

Another example of stereotyping. It's worth reflecting on Dickens's choice of names in the novel. We have already met M'Choakumchild and Gradgrind as examples of those who stifle natural emotion. In the name Harthouse, however, there is a sense of emotion.

GLOSSARY

Graces three sisters who were the personification of charm and beauty in human life (Greek mythology). 'Cutting the throats of the Graces' alludes to the violence done to the idea of beauty

Gradgrind school not a reference to his educational
establishment but to his philosophy or school of thought
yaw-yawed imitation of upper-class mannerisms
hybrid race a mixture of human kind
polonies type of sausage

CHAPTER 3

The whelp

*Notice how the
plot is thickening.*

'The whelp' – a young pup – is what Dickens, speaking
through James Harthouse, calls Tom Gradgrind.
'Whelp', when used to describe a human being, has less
attractive associations. It suggests worthlessness and
underhandedness. And so it proves with Tom, who
becomes putty in the hands of the sophisticated
Harthouse. This chapter shows how Harthouse gathers
information about Louisa, Bounderby, Mrs Sparsit and
Gradgrind from the unsuspecting Tom.

Dickens has earlier mentioned Lucifer when speaking
of Harthouse. Here, he adopts a similar description: 'a
kind of agreeable demon who had only to hover over
him and he must give up his soul if required'. Dickens
has now introduced and is fast developing a further
strand in his story, distinct from the Blackpool/Rachael
story, and, though related to the Gradgrind/Bounderby
strand, still somewhat distinct from that, too.

COMMENT   One important contribution that Harthouse makes is to
enhance the role of Tom Gradgrind. He is shown to be
the gullible victim of Harthouse's subtle, manipulative
character. Tom tries to emulate Harthouse's worldly
ways, and provides us with a degree of humour in the
process. However, this is set in sharp contrast to the
grim forebodings when Dickens says: 'If he had had any
sense of what he had done that night … he might have
turned short on the road, might have gone down to the
ill-smelling river that was dyed black, might have gone
to bed in it for good and all'.

CHAPTER 4

*Men and
brothers*

At a union meeting, Stephen Blackpool is disciplined for refusing to agree to the negotiating terms formulated by the United Aggregate Tribunal. Dickens emphasises the ranting oratory of Slackbridge, the union representative, and contrasts it with the submissive, humble pleas of Stephen to be allowed to work despite his inability to agree with policy. His workmates refuse to work with him, and he cannot bring himself to seek solace from Rachael. In his loneliness, he is approached by Bitzer, identified here only by the description of 'a young man of a very light complexion'. Bitzer tells Blackpool that Bounderby wishes to speak to him.

Bitzer, a minor character, is used as a link between different sets of characters.

COMMENT   The union movement, exemplified by Slackbridge, does not win Dickens's approval (see Context & Setting). It's well illustrated in this treatment of Stephen Blackpool.

Stephen's role as a martyr continues – a victim in his married state, a victim at work, he cries out for sympathy from the reader.

It's important to identify the many forms of exaggeration in Dickens's novel. It's here again in the

Y

portrayal of Slackbridge, in his presentation of Stephen, in his depiction of Harthouse. It is useful to adopt a point of view on this feature of Dickens's novel and say whether you approve or disapprove of it.

GLOSSARY   battened upon   fed like gluttons

he who sold his birthright for a mess of pottage   a reference to the Old Testament story of Esau, who gave up his legal property rights to his brother Jacob for a plate of stew (Genesis 25)

Castlereagh   Robert Stewart Castlereagh (1769–1822), British statesman accused of betraying British interests in Ireland. He eventually committed suicide

moydert   confused

Strike o' day   dawn

fratch   disagreement

Gonnows   God knows

Brutus   Marcus Brutus (c.85–42bc), Roman politician who took part in the murder of Julius Caesar

Spartan mothers   Sparta, a city of ancient Greece, had a military tradition, and its women were bred to become efficient, unfeeling mothers of soldiers

fugleman   the soldier who beat time for a drill

sent to Coventry   disowned and ostracised by workmates

CHAPTER 5
Men and
masters

As at their last meeting, Stephen again finds Bounderby eating. He is now in the company of his wife, Louisa, and her brother Tom and Harthouse. It is significant that when we meet Harthouse again, on this occasion we find him talking to Louisa. He treats Stephen with indifference. Bounderby demands that Blackpool tell them of his dealings with the union – or Combination as he calls it. Stephen is not to be bullied into volunteering opinions about the union; on the contrary, he firmly defends the sincerity of most of its members. Stephen does not, in fact, address his remarks to Bounderby but to Louisa, in whose face he seems to find some sympathy. Bounderby asks him to explain what the workers have to complain about.

Think how disastrous it is for Stephen to lose his job.

Stephen points out that there seems no purpose in their lives. They are born to work in terrible conditions, and then just to die. They are not encouraged to have any hopes or aspirations. In anger, Bounderby says he will crush any threat of rebellion by transporting Slackbridge and his kind as convicts. Stephen replies that this kind of action will not solve the underlying problems. He insists that both parties must be prepared to meet, to compromise and thus reach agreement. They must not maintain their extreme, opposing positions. For his speech, Stephen is sacked on the spot by the enraged Bounderby.

COMMENT   G.K. Chesterton (1874–1936), novelist and critic, once described *Hard Times* as the harshest of Dickens's stories. Note what evidence so far you can provide for that. From this chapter you might instance the plight of Stephen Blackpool: he has a drunken wife from whom he cannot escape; he loves another but cannot marry her; he is disowned by his workmates; he is sacked by his employer. There seems no respite from disaster.

However, there is some relief provided, too, in the shape of Louisa. She extends some sympathy and support to Stephen.

This link between Louisa from one strand of the story and Stephen from another is what we call a plotting device. For it is through that link that Tom can become connected with Stephen and thus carry his own plans forward! You will have noted already how often Tom exploits his sister for his own purposes.

CHAPTER 6

Fading away
Mrs Pegler adds mystery to the novel.

On leaving the house, Stephen meets Rachael in the company of the mysterious old lady he had met in 'The Old Woman' chapter. She is anxious to hear of Bounderby's wife, and is delighted to find that she is 'bonny'. Stephen breaks the news to Rachael that he is finished with Bounderby, and has decided to leave

Coketown and seek his fortune elsewhere. He invites Rachael and the old woman back to his room for a cup of tea, and we learn that his wife has left him again some months ago. We also hear that the old woman's name is Mrs Pegler, that she is a widow and had a son who, it seems, is now dead.

She appears very perturbed when she hears that a Bounderby has come to see Stephen, but this proves to be Louisa and not Josiah. She is accompanied by Tom. She expresses her concern for Stephen's plight and offers him money. Stephen accepts two pounds, but insists that they are only a loan. He plans to leave the area, he tells them, and seek employment elsewhere.

Think whether Tom is really doing him a favour or whether he is going to use him in some awful plan.

Before Louisa and Tom leave, Tom pulls Stephen urgently out of the room and says that he might be able to do him a favour. He tells him to be outside Bounderby's bank at night and wait for an hour or so. He says that if he can help Stephen he will give Bitzer a message for him. He claims that Louisa will agree with what he has in mind, and this single fact seems to persuade Stephen to agree to Tom's request.

Afterwards, Stephen and Rachael see Mrs Pegler to her lodgings, and then they part company. Stephen dutifully spends three nights outside the bank. On the last, he remains there for over two hours, making sure that he is seen by Bitzer in case the latter has a message for him. Nothing happens. The next morning Stephen leaves Coketown alone.

COMMENT

Dickens spells out the lack of any earlier connection with, or even awareness of, Stephen Blackpool by Louisa. It may surprise you that the novel has progressed to this point without that connection!

Again, questions are posed in this chapter: why does Mrs Pegler react in that particular way at the mention

of Bounderby's name? Why does Tom arrange for
Stephen to loiter outside the bank?

We note the presence once again of Bitzer, working in
his new role for Mrs Sparsit and Bounderby. He has
never been a character to admire, and this is now
aggravated by his role as an arch-spy.

GLOSSARY   **Lord Chesterfield** English statesman (1694–1773) best
                remembered for his *Letters to his Son* offering advice and
                worldly wisdom

CHAPTER 7   Louisa and Harthouse are often in one another's
                company – though neither of them has any ulterior
                motive in this. Louisa has a light-hearted attitude to
Gunpowder   life, and to the relationship: 'What did it matter?', and
                Harthouse sees it as part of the 'great fun' that is his
                object in life.

They meet at a new residence taken over by Bounderby
from a bankrupt. It is outside Coketown, in beautiful
countryside. Harthouse intends to gain some kind of
response from Louisa, sees the best way to do this is to
show interest in her brother. So, in his talks with her, he
expresses concern that Tom may have gambling debts.
Louisa volunteers the information that Tom has
borrowed large sums of money from her. Harthouse
expresses sympathy for Tom, saying that his upbringing
has really proved a disadvantage to him, as he has no
Harthouse reveals   one to turn to except his sister. At the same time, he
his deviousness.   says that Tom has not duly recognised how much he
owes to Louisa. He ought to demonstrate some love
and regard for her. It is his intent, he says, to help Tom
himself and, having done so, to be in a position to insist
that he treat Louisa more kindly.

At this point, Tom arrives in an obvious temper.
Harthouse calms him down and, once Louisa has left

them, has a confidential chat with him. He learns that Tom is annoyed that Louisa does not exercise her influence with Bounderby enough to get him more money. He actually breaks down and cries, and Harthouse invites him to confide in him as a friend. He also persuades Tom to be more loving to his sister. In this way Harthouse has effectively won the affections of both brother and sister!

GLOSSARY   **Gorgon** There were three Gorgons, sisters, whose heads were covered with snakes instead of hair, and who, if looked upon, could turn a man to stone (Greek mythology)
Westminster School English public school attached to Westminster Abbey
King's Scholar holder of a scholarship awarded to pupils of high intellectual achievement

CHAPTER 8

Explosion

The aptness of the chapter title becomes obvious when Bounderby tells Harthouse that the bank has been robbed. Bounderby's intention of causing Harthouse alarm by his dramatic announcement fails and Harthouse points out that he was lucky only £150 has gone. Bounderby, however, is not to be calmed. Having been joined by Louisa, Mrs Sparsit and Bitzer, he relates how the money was stolen from Tom Gradgrind's safe the previous night. He says more would have been taken but the thief was disturbed. He would appear to have used a false key. Tom, he says, is being interviewed by police, but the suspect is, in fact, Stephen Blackpool, who was seen loitering outside the bank at night. A second suspect is the old woman who was seen in his company, and who had also been seen watching the bank.

Mrs Sparsit provides a light interlude.

In an amusing interlude, Dickens describes Mrs Sparsit's behaviour in the house. Her main intention is to cause discomfort to Louisa whom she insists on calling Miss Gradgrind. It is she, for example, who draws attention to the fact that Louisa and Harthouse are in the garden together in the evening.

Louisa questions Tom, who has returned from Coketown on the 'mail train'. She obviously suspects him of the robbery and begs him to confess to her. He pretends not to understand what she means. However, his actions when he is left alone in his bedroom will persuade the reader that he is indeed guilty.

COMMENT   Dickens's plotting has been compared to a jigsaw where all the bits and pieces gradually and cleverly come together, each life touching another life. The most impressive example of this is the manner in which the old woman who has been expressing an interest in Bounderby has suddenly become a suspect in the bank robbery.

GLOSSARY   legion possibly a reference to the New Testament story of the man possessed by a devil calling himself Legion (Mark 5: 9). This would be in keeping with Dickens's depiction of Harthouse as something of an evil spirit

the Devil ... lion a direct reference to the New Testament: 'the devil, as a roaring lion, walketh about, seeking whom he may devour'(1 Peter 5: 8)

flying into town on a broomstick Bounderby speaks of the old woman as though she were a witch

CHAPTER 9   There is a growing rift between Louisa and Bounderby, a rift engineered skilfully and deliberately by Mrs *Hearing the* Sparsit. Dickens, though, distracts us from this line of *last of it* the plot by whisking Louisa off to Coketown where her mother is dying. There, looking after her, she finds her sister, Jane, and Sissy. Mr Gradgrind, Dickens tells us, is not there but is in the 'national dustyard', as he calls Parliament. Alone, Louisa witnesses the death of her mother.

Y

COMMENT   Dickens's death scenes enjoy a considerable literary reputation. There is a simplicity about them which removes any sense of insincerity. We are invited to be moved emotionally. The death of Mrs Gradgrind is a classic example: 'the light that had always been feeble and dim behind the weak transparency went out'.

Louisa's reaction to her mother's death is a measure of her developing sensitivity. As if to suggest how much she might have benefited by a closer and continuing association with Sissy Jupe, we are told how much Louisa's sister, Jane, has learned from her influence.

GLOSSARY   consummate velocity high speed
epigrammatically wittily and concisely

CHAPTER 10

Mrs Sparsit's staircase   Mrs Sparsit stays on at Bounderby's and continues to spy on Louisa. We learn that, so far, Blackpool and the 'old woman' have not been found. Meanwhile, Harthouse tries to convince Louisa that Stephen Blackpool was exactly the kind of person to have committed the robbery; he had, as the jargon has it, motive and opportunity.

COMMENT   In the last chapter of Book the First, it was suggested that Mrs Sparsit was not wholly pleased by Bounderby marrying Louisa. Since then her persecution of Louisa has been unceasing. For example, she has insisted on calling her Miss Gradgrind. This chapter focuses on Mrs Sparsit's obsessive contempt for Louisa and her determination to bring about her downfall.

GLOSSARY   retreat Bounderby's country house – a place to escape from the dirt and noise of Coketown
anchorite hermit
Mahommedan persuasion belief in Mohammed the prophet (c.570–632)

to hear is to obey Mohammed's response to God's call

allegorical fancy an imaginative picture (in this case 'a mighty Staircase') which acts as a symbol (see Literary Terms)

Romulus and Remus the legendary founders of Rome supposedly nurtured by a she-wolf

Alderney one of the Channel Islands, famous for its breed of cows. Bounderby suggests that, just as an Alderney cow is prolific in its milk production so his grandmother was unstinting in giving blows and bruises

under the rose sub rosa: secretly

CHAPTER 11

Lower and lower

Mrs Sparsit the busybody becomes Mrs Sparsit the spy!

Mrs Sparsit's insane jealousy of Louisa has now reached dramatic proportions, with frenetic attempts to spy on Louisa and Harthouse. But they are not so frenetic that they cannot be calculating. She learns from Tom that he is to meet Harthouse at the station on his return from Yorkshire. At the same time, she learns that Bounderby is not to be at home that same weekend. She anticipates that a plan has been laid by Harthouse to meet Louisa at the house, and this suspicion is confirmed when she sees that Harthouse has not arrived at the station to meet Tom. She sets off immediately to Bounderby's house and there, as she hides in the shrubbery, she witnesses the encounter between Harthouse and Louisa. It starts to rain heavily and the couple part. Mrs Sparsit guesses that they have a further assignation and decides to follow Louisa. This entails pursuing her to Coketown, travelling in the same train. But, once in Coketown, Louisa disappears.

COMMENT

The preoccupation with Mrs Sparsit continues. She has suddenly become almost a major character in the novel.

In addition, the focus here has shifted from concerns about industrialisation to a mixture of detective story and romance. The first element of the detective story had been the hunt for Stephen Blackpool; the new strand is Mrs Sparsit's single-handed pursuit of the secret of Louisa and Harthouse.

GLOSSARY   **small fry** literally, small young fish, but here the less important people in the factory
                  Furies female figures who tortured the conscience of evil-doers (Greek mythology)

CHAPTER 12

Down

The literalness of this chapter's heading is made clear in the last sentence: 'And he laid her down there, and saw the pride of his heart and the triumph of his system, lying, an insensible heap, at his feet'. This is a dramatic conclusion to the Second Book, the climax to Louisa's heart-searching confession to her father. For it is to her father's house that Louisa has gone, not, as Mrs Sparsit suspected, to the arms of James Harthouse. Once there, Louisa accuses her father of neglecting the real needs of her heart and soul in her upbringing. All that Gradgrind can say in his defence is that he did not know that she was unhappy.

COMMENT

The drama of Harthouse's pursuit of Louisa is represented in two ways. One is the sense of climax in Louisa's arrival at her father's house; the other is in the nature of the lengthy dialogue between the two characters that dominates this episode.

Gradgrind's reactions to Louisa's confession enhance our estimate of his character, in a way that sharply contrasts with our last impressions of him, when he agreed that she should marry Bounderby. He is also a different man to the one who, at the start of the novel, preferred facts to the world of the imagination.

GLOSSARY   **Good Samaritan** a reference to the New Testament story (Luke 10: 30–5) where a man gave help to a stranger in need

A *Identify the speaker.*

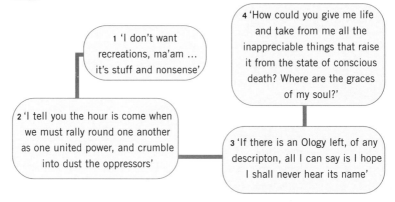

1 'I don't want recreations, ma'am ... it's stuff and nonsense'

4 'How could you give me life and take from me all the inappreciable things that raise it from the state of conscious death? Where are the graces of my soul?'

2 'I tell you the hour is come when we must rally round one another as one united power, and crumble into dust the oppressors'

3 'If there is an Ology left, of any descripton, all I can say is I hope I shall never hear its name'

Identify the person 'to whom' this comment refers.

5 He held the respectable office of general spy and informer in the establishment

6 'He is a dissipated, extravagant idler. he is not worth his salt, ma'am'

Check your answers on page 85.

 B *Consider these issues.*

a How the depiction of Bitzer suits the theme of the novel that, 'As ye sow, so shall ye reap'.

b How sadness is created in this part of the novel.

c Whether the novel has suddenly changed its emphasis in any way. Whether, for example, it has simply become an adventure story.

d The part played by coincidence in this story.

BOOK THE THIRD: GARNERING

CHAPTER 1

Another thing needful

This chapter depicts the struggle in Louisa's mind. Years of training in restraining herself and repressing her emotions have made it difficult for her to experience any feelings for her father or Sissy or her sister, Jane. Her father's appeals to her threaten to fall even now on deaf ears. Dickens tells us that 'he would have been glad to see her in tears' but the tears will not come. She visibly resists Sissy's good influence and sees her as her enemy. It is only when Sissy's tears touch Louisa's cheeks that she finds in herself the gifts of tears and breaks down, held against Sissy's 'loving heart'.

COMMENT

Note the comment Dickens makes that 'All closely imprisoned forces rend and destroy'. Dickens is talking here about the dangers of being repressed, a psychological time-bomb. He is suggesting that if we do not release and express our emotions we shall destroy ourselves. His particular concern is about the mental state of Louisa. Watch her struggle and finally see her win control over her new self.

Note the dramatic change, too, in Thomas Gradgrind, who is now shown to be sensitive and even humble. He is certainly a different character to the arrogant and pompous Gradgrind of the first part of the novel.

GLOSSARY

excise-rod device used by Customs to measure whisky and other spirits

CHAPTER 2

Very ridiculous

The bemused James Harthouse is disturbed by Louisa's unexplained absence. He searches for her and questions Tom as to her whereabouts. Tom is uncharacteristically aggressive and points out that he has experienced considerable annoyance himself in waiting to meet Harthouse at the station the previous evening.

By contrast, Harthouse is fully relaxed even though he is puzzled as to what has happened to Louisa.

Y

Garnering

The chapter title is   That night, Harthouse has a visit from Sissy who
an apt description   persuades him that he will never see Louisa again and
of this episode.   encourages him to leave the district. After a token
protest, Harthouse agrees to do so, and, leaving a note
for Bounderby and Gradgrind, 'he left the tall chimneys
of Coketown behind'.

Comment   Check how often Dickens asks you willingly to accept
what is, perhaps, a little far-fetched: here, for example,
James Harthouse's readiness to listen to Sissy Jupe's
pleas for him to leave Coketown and never see
Louisa again.

Note yet another reference to Harthouse's 'devilishness',
when he tells us that he has 'glided on from one step to
another with a smoothness so perfectly diabolical'.

In this final section, think about the role played by
Sissy Jupe throughout, especially the miraculous change
she has brought about in James Harthouse. Note, too,
that despite changes in other characters' behaviour,
Sissy Jupe remains totally consistent.

GLOSSARY   **Holy Office and slow torture** the trial and torture of heretics by
the Spanish Inquisition of the fifteenth and sixteenth centuries
addled eggs stale eggs that produce no young

CHAPTER 3   Mrs Sparsit, a shadow of her former self, seeks out Mr
Bounderby in London and tells him her tale. Having
Very decided done so, she faints from exhaustion. In dramatic style,
Bounderby whisks her back to Coketown and to Stone
Lodge for a confrontation with Thomas Gradgrind.
Gradgrind acknowledges that he knows the story
already and is able to set the record straight.

When Bounderby hears of Louisa's flight from
Harthouse to her father, he turns on Mrs Sparsit and
demands an apology. She bursts into tears and he packs
her off abruptly back to the bank.

Things happen at great speed after this. Bounderby attacks Thomas Gradgrind's protective attitude towards Louisa and lays down an ultimatum: that if she is not at home with him by noon the next day she need never return. Since Louisa fails to meet the deadline, Bounderby resumes 'the bachelor life'.

COMMENT   The favourable presentation of Thomas Gradgrind continues. He even confesses to a doubt 'whether I understood Louisa'. By contrast, we see how Bounderby and Sparsit remain unchanged. The latter is now totally disgraced, though; yet we shall see (in Chapter 5) that she is still capable of making an even greater fool of herself.

Bounderby's effective divorce of Louisa is in sharp contrast to the strict moral attitude he struck with Stephen Blackpool in Book the First, where he had said that the severing of ties between man and wife was unthinkable!

GLOSSARY   combustibles things that catch fire easily – a cross reference to the 'Gunpowder' chapter

Rocket George Stephenson's (1781–1848) steam engine 'The Rocket', built in 1829

jerk in the hayfield jerk of the head. Dickens has already described Bounderby's almost bald head as a hayfield

CHAPTER 4   Stephen Blackpool's whereabouts suddenly become the focus of attention. Bounderby, with renewed energy,
Lost   since his rift with Louisa, offers a reward of £20 for his 'apprehension'. This gives rise to a further denunciation of Bounderby by Slackbridge, and to an outburst by Rachael. She protests Stephen's innocence to Bounderby and tells him of the visit to Stephen's lodgings of Tom and Louisa. Bounderby insists that she and Tom should see Louisa at Stone Lodge with him and gain corroboration of Rachael's story.

Despite obvious hints from Tom when we reach Stone Lodge, Louisa confirms Rachael's account. We learn that Rachael has been writing to Stephen Blackpool who now has an assumed name. She assures them that Stephen will return to Coketown within two days. But Stephen does not appear. Rachael is forced to tell of his whereabouts, and messengers are sent to bring him back. He is not, however, to be found.

COMMENT

One frequently used principle of Dickens's story-telling technique is to make us wait, and he does so again here. Stephen's return to Coketown would have solved the mystery of the robbery. Rachael has told of his whereabouts yet, when they seek him, he has disappeared again.

The trials that Tom and his father have endured have taken their toll physically. Tom is becoming ill, and Thomas has grown 'grey and old'. They are paying the penalty for their misguided actions and attitudes. We note, by contrast, how the good and the innocent like Rachael are still blessed by looking young.

CHAPTER 5

Found

Blackpool's whereabouts are still not known, and Rachael fears he may have been murdered. Sissy suggests that he may have fallen ill on his way back, but Rachael says all possibilities have been exhausted.

Notice how Mrs Sparsit makes an even greater fool of herself.

Whilst walking together they witness a commotion outside Bounderby's house. At the centre of it is Mrs Sparsit who is in the process of dragging an old woman out of a coach in which she has been brought from the railway station. She is hustled into Bounderby's house, followed by Rachael and Sissy and a great many of the townspeople. There, in a triumphant moment, Mrs Sparsit delivers the old woman thought to have been Stephen's accomplice, to Bounderby. He is, however, none too pleased, and asks Mrs Sparsit, 'Why

Y

don't you mind your own business, ma'am?' For the old woman, it would appear, is his mother!

Gradgrind, also present, rounds on the old woman and abuses her for her neglect of her son as a child – a story Bounderby has persistently related throughout. She is horrified by this, and denies the truth of it vehemently. Bounderby is rightly embarrassed by Mrs Pegler's account and orders everyone out of his house.

COMMENT   Dickens plays a little trick on his readers by his choice of chapter title. We could be forgiven for thinking that it was the 'lost' Stephen Blackpool who had been discovered. Instead, it is Bounderby's mother. This has the added beauty of keeping us in suspense a little longer about the fate of Stephen Blackpool.

GLOSSARY   **Slough of Despond** a place of despair described in John Bunyan's Pilgrim's Progress (1678)

CHAPTER 6

The starlight

On the Sunday following the discovery of Mrs Pegler's true identity, Sissy and Rachael go for a walk about seven miles from Coketown. They are in green countryside which, however, still shows the scars of industry in the shape of deserted mines. It is, indeed, into one of these disused pits that Stephen has fallen.

Sissy first finds his hat lying on the ground. Rachael becomes hysterical. Sissy has to calm her sufficiently to persuade her to run for help.

Notice how Stephen's life is tragic to the end.

Meanwhile Sissy organises a search party to look for Stephen in Old Hell Shaft. It takes four hours for the rescue operation to get underway. There are then almost 200 spectators. Two men are lowered into the pit, and news comes through that Stephen is still alive but so badly hurt that he cannot easily be moved. Eventually, however, he is raised to the surface. Once there, he has the chance to speak to Rachael, Louisa and Thomas Gradgrind. He still insists that it is 'aw a muddle', but that he has become resigned to that. He asks Gradgrind to clear his name, and, holding Rachael's hand, he dies.

COMMENT

Wherever Stephen Blackpool appears there is bound to be action and tension. We found it in the union episode, in his confrontation with Bounderby over the question of divorce, and in his naïve role in Tom's plot. In this chapter he steals the scene again by dying dramatically and, before doing so, clearing his good name.

The death scene with all its sadness reminds us of the other death scene of Mrs Gradgrind. Dickens is very fond of such sentimental effects and enhances it in this case by Rachael's reaction, and the fact that Stephen finally has so many mourners. Most important, perhaps, are Stephen's own reflections on his life, namely, that it is 'aw a muddle'. Be sure that that philosophy does not affect your own approach to the reading of the events in this book! You must be sure that all the strands are clear to you.

GLOSSARY

Fire-damp a hazard to miners, carburetted hydrogen is explosive when it mingles with air

Y

CHAPTER 7

Whelp-hunting

Gradgrind realises Tom's responsibility for Stephen's death and loss of good name. Sissy has alerted Tom and helped him to escape by encouraging him to join Sleary's circus. The circus happens to be within reach of the port of Liverpool, and so Tom could escape from the country by ship. Thomas Gradgrind, Louisa and Sissy go their separate ways in search of Tom. Sissy and Louisa are the first to find Sleary's circus. Tom has been disguised as a black servant in one of the acts and is unrecognisable. Mr Gradgrind arrives an hour later and arrangements are made to get Tom to Liverpool. Before this can be effected, however, Bitzer bursts in on the scene and arrests Tom.

COMMENT

Note the irony (see Literary Terms) of this chapter. The circus that had been a subject of contempt for the old Thomas Gradgrind has now become the only means for him to save his son. The man who had originally objected to any kind of decoration is now glad to see his son disguised as a black servant.

We have commented on Dickens's continued use of apparently minor characters. It is in evidence again here with the reappearance of Bitzer, whose role is to arrest Tom. We can believe that Bitzer's approach to the definition of a horse will be the same at this stage of the novel as at the beginning. Like Sissy Jupe, he has never changed.

GLOSSARY

down wells an ironic (see Literary Terms) picture in view of the events in the previous chapter – it means here, though, stairwells at the bottom of steep staircases

postilion outrider of a horse-drawn carriage

kicking a horse in a fly the old man is kicking the horse which is supposed to draw the carriage (the fly)

turnpike-road a road on which tolls must be paid

grown too maturely turfy he had grown a beard!

CHAPTER 8

Philosophical

*Gradgrind sees
that Bitzer is
motivated entirely
by self-interest.*

When it seems that all hope of escape for Tom is lost, Sleary devises another plan. Pretending to sympathise with Bitzer's point of view, he offers to take him with Tom to the railway station. But the horse that draws the carriage in which they ride has been trained to dance, and Sleary's dog has been ordered to detain Bitzer. The plan is that, when the horse begins dancing, Tom will know that a pony-gig is due to pass. When that happens he is to jump from the carriage and get into the gig which will take him to safety. Bitzer will be prevented from pursuing him by Sleary's dog. The horse will go on dancing for as long as Sleary wishes.

Thus, Tom makes his escape. For this service Sleary accepts some small rewards from Thomas Gradgrind. In talking of his own dog, Sleary is prompted to tell Gradgrind of the sudden and unexpected appearance of Sissy Jupe's dog, Merrylegs. Signor Jupe is never heard of again, and Sleary thinks it is certain that he is dead.

COMMENT

Given the comment on the nature of horses as seen by Bitzer, the behaviour of Sleary's horse seems even more significant here!

Dickens has stretched our willingness to believe to the limits more than once in this novel. It's worth considering whether this last demand on our credulity is the most daring or not! You might think that performing dogs and horses in a circus context are perfectly believable.

GLOSSARY

Harvey William Harvey (1578–1657), English anatomist who discovered the circulation of blood

CHAPTER 9

Final

Mrs Sparsit falls from her exalted position when Bounderby discharges her without ceremony, and she has to seek refuge under the roof of her 'relation, Lady Scadgers'. Having dealt with her, Dickens offers us a

y

look into the future of each of his leading characters. Mr Bounderby did, in fact, give Bitzer Tom's place in the bank, and made a will offering certain bequests to glorify his own name. Dickens ruefully comments that the law will make due profit out of the contesting of his will.

Notice how neatly Dickens ties up all the loose ends of the novel.

Gradgrind grows to old age, having renounced his factual approach to life and having given up Parliament.

Louisa helps her father to exonerate Stephen Blackpool; she never remarries, but lives quietly, helping her fellow-men.

Rachael, for her part, continues working and, ironically (see Literary Terms), helps to support Stephen's wife on her occasional drunken visits to Coketown.

Tom Gradgrind, thousands of miles away, becomes a reformed character and learns the value of humanity. He starts on a journey back to England but dies of fever on the way.

Sissy Jupe becomes the happy mother of happy children.

COMMENT   The final chapter of a Victorian novel was often used as a kind of summary of what happened to all the leading characters after the main story has been told. Dickens uses this convention and all his surviving characters are given a new life. Justice in each case is seen to be done, and troubles seem to have ended. Where they still seem to exist – as in the case of Stephen's drunken wife – there is always a good person to deal with it.

A Identify the speaker.

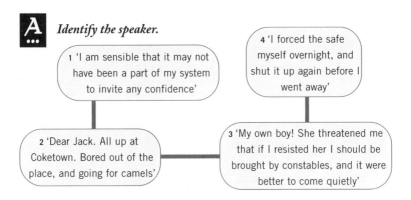

1 'I am sensible that it may not have been a part of my system to invite any confidence'

4 'I forced the safe myself overnight, and shut it up again before I went away'

2 'Dear Jack. All up at Coketown. Bored out of the place, and going for camels'

3 'My own boy! She threatened me that if I resisted her I should be brought by constables, and it were better to come quietly'

Identify the person 'to whom' this comment refers.

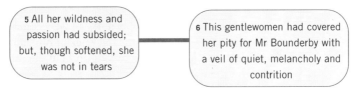

5 All her wildness and passion had subsided; but, though softened, she was not in tears

6 This gentlewomen had covered her pity for Mr Bounderby with a veil of quiet, melancholy and contrition

Check your answers on page 85.

B Consider these issues.

a Whether there is any comedy in this part of the book. If so, what purpose it serves.

b How convincing the interview is between Sissy Jupe and Harthouse.

c To what extent the principal characters have changed in the course of the novel.

d Think about what you see as the purpose of the final chapter of the novel.

e How well the title 'All is Revealed' would suit the contents of this part of the book.

PART THREE

COMMENTARY

THEMES

EDUCATION   The opening schoolroom scene brings us straight to
one of the novel's most significant themes.

This schoolroom is described as 'a plain, bare,
monotonous vault'. There is no room for any decoration
in this classroom, any more than there is room for

Dickens is critical   imagination in the training of the scholars. The
of this dull   emphasis is on 'Facts'. The principle of education, we are
approach to   told, is to fill 'the little pitchers' (the children) with facts.
education which
consists of facts,   When some interest in the imagination is expressed, it
with no use of   is quickly suppressed. Sissy Jupe is told: 'You are never
imagination.   to fancy'.

Dickens's view of this depressing approach to education
is fittingly summed up in the name he gives the
children's teacher Mr M'Choakumchild. There is a total
neglect of the development of sensibilities. This is not
confined to schooling. It affects home and family.

Dickens contrasts this with the colourful and rich life of
the imagination experienced by the circus folk. The
central theme is the conflict of Fact and Fancy in
children's education. Where failure occurs in adult life,
it is inevitable that this should be attributed to the
inadequacy of early childhood experiences.

INDUSTRY   Just as Dickens's educational theme is startlingly
summarised in his graphic description of the school
environment, so his depiction of industrialisation is
unforgettably presented through his picture of
Coketown in 'The Key-note' chapter: He never tires of
repeating such descriptions, and the squalor of the
industrial environment is graphically presented in his

account of 'the innermost fortifications of that ugly
citadel where Nature was as strongly bricked out as
killing airs and gases were bricked in … where the
chimneys, for want of air to make a draught, were built
in an immense variety of stunted and crooked shapes'
('Stephen Blackpool' chapter).

It is, finally, in the words of the dying Stephen
Blackpool that Dickens condemns the abuses of
industrialisation: 'I ha' fell into a pit that ha' been wi'
the fire-damp crueller than battle. I ha' read on't in a
public petition … fro' the men that works in pits, in
which they ha' pray'n and pray'n the lawmakers for
Christ's sake not to let their work be murder to 'em'.

*Think about
whether the pit
into which
Stephen falls is
symbolic and what
it symbolises*

Through Stephen Blackpool, too, Dickens has provided
another angle on industrialisation through his portrayal
of the conflict between trade unions and factory
managers. Dickens, as we know, visited Preston (a town
near Blackpool!) to report on a strike. In his article 'On
Strike' (published in *Household Words*), Dickens wrote:
'I believe that into the relations between employers
and employed, as with all relations of this life, there
must enter something of feeling and sentiment,
something of mutual explanation, forbearance, and
consideration'. Such sentiments help explain why he
does not seem to take sides either with the factory
owners or the strikers in *Hard Times*. The strike leader
is described in unflattering terms as 'an ill-made, high-
shouldered man, with lowering brows, and his features
crushed into an habitually sour expression'. This can be
seen as counterbalancing the equally unattractive
description of the employer Bounderby   (see
Characters).

MONEY

Interestingly enough, Slackbridge is not negotiating for
increases in wages. Ironically (see Literary Terms), part
of his appeal in the 'Men and Brothers' chapter is for

y

money. He claims it will be a mark of triumph for the workers 'to subscribe to the funds of the United Aggregate Tribunal'.

Stephen is not only financially deprived – he is also deprived of love.

Financial matters are, of course, equally high on the agenda of the employer, Josiah Bounderby. When Stephen comes innocently to him seeking moral guidance on divorce, Bounderby immediately thinks he is seeking some kind of financial reward. 'I see traces of the turtle soup, and venison, and gold spoon in this', he tells Stephen. And he reduces the whole business of marriage and divorce to that level of financial possibilities. He informs Stephen: 'But it's not for you at all. It costs money. It costs a mint of money.'

When it comes to the matter of the eventual divorce from Louisa, it is significant that Bounderby disowns her financially. He tells her father, 'Since you are of opinion that she ought to have what she wants, I recommend you to provide it for her!'

Money is at the heart of the sub-plot to this story. For Tom Gradgrind's robbing the bank provides a further strand to the plot. His need for immediate cash is prompted by his gambling debts. Gambling will have been judged to be an immoral act, worthy of someone whose childhood had been marred by lack of generosity of spirit. As Dickens says in the final chapter, even the national prosperity figures rely on such 'imaginative graces and delights'.

FAMILY

The novel concentrates on several families. The Gradgrinds are dominated very much by a patriarchal figure who dictates the lifestyles of two of his children, Tom and Louisa, and his sickly wife. Watch the gradual disintegration of that family. Tom falls into debt and begins to cheat and lie his way out of it, until he is finally forced to seek exile. Louisa, robbed of all true sentiment, agrees to marry a man she does not love.

*Note how there
are no happy
families here.*
Mrs Gradgrind dies and her last words are words of
complaint about her husband's insistence on empty
learning. Thomas Gradgrind himself has finally to face
the reality of this splintered family through the words
of Louisa, who in 'Down' faces her father with the
harshness of her upbringing: 'your philosophy and your
teaching will not save me. Now, father, you have
brought me to this'.

The family was sacred to the Victorian way of life, and
so the sight of one crumbling to pieces in this way
would be seen as the greatest of tragedies.

The Gradgrind philosophy of 'Facts, Facts, Facts' is
always seen as a sharp contrast to that of the world of
imagination embraced and encouraged by the circus
folk. Yet even there we see again a family in ruins. Sissy
Jupe, held up as a model of fancy and imagination and,
therefore, of a balanced personality, has already lost her
mother and, early on, is abandoned by her father. In
other words, Dickens does not seem to be encouraging
the necessity for family values in rearing children!

Indeed, wherever we look in this novel, the family unit
is threatened. Stephen Blackpool is in misery because of
his estrangement from his drunken wife; Bounderby has
disowned his mother. It is only in the closing pages that
Dickens seems to applaud the blessing of family life, a
blessing that would never be Louisa's but would be
Sissy Jupe's with 'all [her] children loving her; she,
grown learned in childish lore; thinking no innocent
and pretty fancy ever to be despised'.

STRUCTURE

This novel's careful structure is easily illustrated by its
division into three parts that immediately suggest a
pattern. 'Sowing' the seed will eventually lead to 'reaping'
and, finally, to 'garnering' the produce. So the structure
of *Hard Times* is a structure of cause and effect.

Sowing

Spring

Louisa is 15 or 16

Bounderby is 47 or 48

**Time elapses
(shown by Cissy
Jupes's progress
or lack of progress
at school)**

Stephen Blackpool is 40,
although always known as
'old Stephen'

Stephen's drunken wife
returns to him

Stephen seeks Mr
Bounderby's advice

An old woman, Mrs Pegler,
appears outside
Bounderby's house

**'Time went on'
(p.93)**

'Louisa is becoming almost
a young woman.' She
is 20 (p.101)

Sissy Jupe has now left
school (p. 94)

Thomas Gradgrind is
now an MP

Tom goes to work for
Mr Bounderby

Bounderby, now around 50,
proposes to Louisa

**Eight weeks later
they marry**

Reaping

Summer
one year
later

James Harthouse,
aged 35, appears

Tom Gradgrind has
gambling debts

Tom tries to get Harthouse
interested in Louisa

Stephen is 'sent to
Coventry' for not making a
promise to his workmates

Stephen is sacked
by Bounderby

At Tom's request Stephen
waits outside the bank
for three days

Mrs Pegler visits Rachael
and Stephen;
so does Louisa

Stephen leaves Coketown

Three days later

Tom's safe is 'robbed'
at the bank

Bounderby suspects
Stephen

Mrs Gradgrind dies

Harthouse makes improper
advances to Louisa

Louisa seeks refuge from
Harthouse at her father's

Garnering

Early
autumn

Louisa convalesces
at Gradgrind's

Sissy Jupe persuades
Harthouse to leave

The Bounderby marriage is
over, and he sells his
property outside the town

Weeks pass

Bounderby makes Stephen
a 'wanted man'

Rachael sends for Stephen

A week passes

Stephen does not return

Mrs Pegler's identity
is revealed

**On a Sunday
in September**

Stephen is found down
a disused mineshaft

Tom's guilt is public

Tom escapes through
the good offices of
Sleary's circus

That suggests, too, that Dickens's novel is strictly chronological in structure. The novel opens with a classroom of children, follows the development of four of them into adulthood, and ends with a new generation of children whose future is to be so much more enlightened.

Dickens's artistry is in using one plot to create suspense in another, by making the reader wait.

Once the plot is established, Dickens introduces a second plot, relating to the plight of Stephen Blackpool in his marriage and in his workplace. We follow his sorry state in his attempts to negotiate some way in which to deal with both.

However, Dickens's skill as an artist is nicely demonstrated when he effects a link between these apparently separate plots. He did this, initially, by having Louisa marry Josiah Bounderby. Thus the theme of education is immediately linked with that of industrialisation. Louisa becomes involved with Stephen Blackpool through her charitable concern for him and Rachael and the drunken wife. Tom, on his part, becomes linked with Stephen through his plotting to rob the bank.

This particular device of linking these plot-lines establish the novel's strong claims to be seen as a work of art. It's worth contrasting its cleverness and coherence with Stephen's own experience of the world as 'aw a muddle'.

In *Hard Times* paths cross and criss-cross with remarkable ease. Thus, for example, the meeting of Mrs Pegler and Stephen outside Bounderby's house in 'The Old Woman' (Book the First), and again in 'Fading Away' (Book the Second), prove crucial to the robbery.

The structure is enhanced by the persistence of themes and of characters. In many a Dickens novel minor characters sink without trace. In *Hard Times* people like

Dickens uses minor characters to link the different plots.

Bitzer and Mrs Pegler are permanent fixtures helping to support the whole structure.

Dickens produced *Hard Times* under pressure of time. He published it in serial form in his magazine *Household Words*. A chapter or two appeared each week for a period of five months. Given that kind of pressure it is not surprising that the end-product was, in fact, so closely knit. The characters, themes, and plot-lines were obviously part of his every waking moment over those five months!

CHARACTERS

THOMAS GRADGRIND

A heavy father
Kindly
Blinkered

Father to Tom, Louisa, Jane, Malthus, and Adam Smith; becomes an MP; severe to his children; believes in 'Facts'.

No name seems to reward our attention so much in *Hard Times* as that of Gradgrind, with all its connotations of slavish attention to petty detail – the 'grind' – and its concern with the different stages of our lives – the 'grade' or 'grad'. Because of his insistence that his children should attend to factual matters alone, they are in danger of never developing fully as people.

However, Gradgrind is not all bad. It was he who offered Sissy a home. And this action was very much against the advice and wish of Bounderby, who saw in it a threat to Louisa and Tom. And, indeed, this action does have a profound effect on Louisa and on the other members of the Gradgrind family.

In many ways, Dickens is sympathetic towards Gradgrind. He never attributes ill-will to him and Gradgrind never hurts anyone intentionally. Louisa, whom we may well regard as the victim of her father, assures him, 'I have never blamed you and I never shall'. But there is some ambivalence in Dickens's depiction of Gradgrind. For, having observed in the beginning of Book the Third a distinct change of heart in him, we then find, in Chapter 5 of the same book, that he has become supportive of Bounderby and even somewhat dictatorial. Our unfavourable impression of him in this one episode, however, is fully offset by his later forgiving attitude towards Tom, and his wish to help him escape punishment. That, indeed, is a change from the Gradgrind who would have penalised his children for stealing a peep at a circus.

JOSIAH BOUNDERBY

Pompous factory owner; cruel to Stephen Blackpool; ugly in appearance; disowns his own mother; marries the young Louisa when he is twice her age; dies in a fit in the gutter.

When reading Dickens we are always looking for some significance in the names he gives his characters. Is Bounderby so named because he was by nature a bounder, a cheat, a deceiver who seeks advancement at the expense of others? In fact, 'Bounder' was Dickens's original choice of name for him.

Self-complacent
Self-made
Repellent
Bully

Dickens condemns Bounderby from the start by his calculated description: 'A man with a great puffed head and forehead, swelled veins in his temples, and such strained skin to his face that it seemed to hold his eyes open and lift his eyebrows up'.

This follows immediately after Gradgrind has threatened Louisa with Bounderby's displeasure. By creating the link between Bounderby and Louisa, between old age and youth, Dickens reinforces this repulsive effect. She marries him out of a sense of duty to her family and not through feelings of love.

Bounderby is boastful and full of bluster. Think whether he has any sympathetic qualities at all.

Bounderby's self-complacency is one of his more unattractive qualities. He is assured that he is worthy of respect and esteem because he is a self-made man. It is his constant boast that he made his own way in the world and achieved success without the help of anyone. He sees himself, too, as a benefactor to his employees. Those two features are given expression in his first conversation with Harthouse: 'I'll state a fact to you. It's the pleasantest work there is, and it's the lightest work there is .... So now we may shake hands on equal terms. I say, equal terms, because although I know what I am, and the exact depth of the gutter I have lifted myself out of ... I am as proud as you are.'

Of course, the inaccuracy of the first part of what he says is blatantly clear, and the untruth of the second is dramatically revealed later when his mother identifies herself.

There is not a single redeeming feature in Bounderby's character. He is, as Dickens frequently describes him, a 'bully'. None of the goodness in the novel ever affects him. Even the presence of both Sissy and Rachael has no effect on him. Dickens does appear to bring him low by his mother's revelations, but we are bound to believe that he will survive even that.

Note how Dickens metes out a horrible end to a horrible character.

He is, however, to be humiliated at the moment of his death, for he dies in a fit in the street. He had hoped to make sure through his will that his name would always be honoured, but Dickens tells us that the law – for which Bounderby claimed to have such admiration – would effectively turn his plan into an unrealised dream, and the only ones who would gain would be the lawyers!

TOM GRADGRIND

Brother to Louisa; exploits other people like her and Stephen Blackpool; robs a bank; has gambling debts; forced into exile; a sad and lonely man.

From the beginning, Tom is drawn as someone who will readily use people. He abuses Louisa's blind devotion in order to serve his own purposes. He frequently encourages her to please Bounderby so that he can gain favours from him. At another point, he uses Stephen Blackpool to help him, unwittingly, to rob the bank. Finally, he is dependent on a whole host of characters to help him escape the clutches of the law.

Exploits others
Sullen & selfish

He is intent on gaining some revenge for the upbringing he had to endure: 'I mean, I'll enjoy myself a little, and go about and see something, and hear something. I'll recompense myself for the way in which I have been brought up' ('Never Wonder').

He incurs heavy gambling debts and is forced to steal from the bank. That he is not a natural thief, however, is made clear by the frightened behaviour he shows after the robbery, for example, in his meeting with James Harthouse ('Gunpowder'):

> 'Tom, what's the matter?'
> 'Oh! Mr Harthouse', said Tom, with a groan, 'I am hard up, and bothered out of my life … I am in a horrible mess'.

His greatest humiliation, though, is, ultimately, to be found disguised as a black servant 'in a preposterous coat'. Dickens has made his own feelings towards Tom abundantly clear in his descriptions of him as a 'whelp'. This cowering, hangdog appearance becomes a feature of his make-up: 'He had long been a down-looking young fellow, but this characteristic had so increased of late, that he never raised his eyes to any face for three seconds together'.

Dickens does not report that Tom repents and is reformed during his enforced exile, but he does not let him live to show that face again in England.

LOUISA GRADGRIND

Louisa is one of the older children in the Gradgrind family, and the main plot revolves around her. She is Tom's sister. She marries Bounderby when she is eighteen, falls in love with Harthouse, is kind and helpful to Stephen Blackpool, lacks emotional expression, is protective towards Tom, and finally learns to deal with her emotions. Her father regards her as the exemplar in his family. When, for example, he catches her and Tom stealing a peep at the circus, his reaction is 'what would your best friend say, Louisa?' His remarks are not addressed to Tom. And, indeed, on this occasion as on others, she speaks for both the children. She defends their presence at the circus unashamedly, for she 'wanted to see what it was like'. She defends Tom against any attack by his father by declaring that she persuaded him to accompany her.

Think about whether you can have any sympathy for Louisa.

She is a precocious child. She treats the pompous Bounderby with contempt even early in the novel when he insists on a kiss from her. And, in the same episode, she amply demonstrates how dead she is to all feeling. Dead to all, that is, except her love for Tom. She would do anything for him. It is a measure of her moral development that she is finally courageous enough to choose truth rather than foolishly protect him.

Through her, Dickens exemplifies the failure of education, as practised by Gradgrind, to develop sensibilities and emotions. Because of this immaturity

Note how Louisa gradually matures. she seems an easy victim to James Harthouse. But, for all the harm Harthouse may have done, he effects some good. It is an ironic (see Literary Terms) result of his attentions to Louisa that she finally sees the relevance of emotions. Hence, when called to her mother's death-bed in 'Hearing the Last of It', she shows herself newly capable of unselfish affection:

> 'I want to hear of you mother; not of myself.'
> 'You want to hear of me, my dear? That's something new.'

Earlier, Dickens had indicated that there were possible depths to her character. She spends many quiet hours looking into the firelight and imagining many things. She has the gift of 'wondering', of imagination. But, whenever this reveals itself, it is repressed by external pressures. She herself even resists any full expression of it – hence her rejection of Sissy's influence early on and her acceptance of Bounderby's proposal of marriage. This act is easily seen as a triumph of the cynicism and despair in her nature.

SISSY JUPE

Angelic
Imaginative

Daughter to Signor Jupe, a circus performer; imaginative; a support for all; persuades James Harthouse to leave Coketown and Louisa; grows up to be a mother.

Sissy belongs to a long line of Dickens's heroines. They are inevitably as pure as can be, angels on earth. Their influence is everywhere benign. From the time Sissy appears she is identified with heavenly light: the 'ray of sunlight', we are told, 'irradiated Sissy'. From the beginning, she is subjected to various trials both at school and home, first bullying in the classroom, a bullying that pursues her in the shape of Bitzer outside the classroom, and at home. Her father abandons her to her fate, and she waits patiently but in vain for him to return. She waits with oils to soothe him after his journey. This role as one who soothes and cures is to be a major one for Sissy. She brings salve to each, even to the cynical James Harthouse. Tom says that she hates him but it is impossible to believe that she could hate anyone.

Yet, though she has high spiritual qualities, she is seen to be in touch with earthly realities, too. When Tom Gradgrind is incriminated by Stephen's dying words it is Sissy who rescues him by telling him to hide in Sleary's circus.

Sissy's influence touches all, it seems. She comforts Rachael whilst she waits for Stephen to return to Coketown and is directly involved in the discovery of the dying Stephen.

STEPHEN BLACKPOOL

Born loser
Tragic

Only forty, but spoken of as 'old Stephen', he has an unfortunate marriage from which he cannot escape; he is a failure at work; loves Rachael but cannot marry her; is suspected of having robbed a bank; dies after falling down a mine-shaft.

The most damning comment on Stephen is made by James Harthouse in 'Mrs Sparsit's Staircase'. In conversation with Louisa, he speaks of him as 'an infinitely dreary person … Lengthy and prosy in the extreme'. The description is not inappropriate. Though Dickens tells us that Stephen's own assessment of his situation was that he had only 'a peck of trouble' the impression he conveys with monotonous regularity is one of carrying a dreadful weight of sorrow. Of course, the reader is bound to sympathise with 'old Stephen' – but he does test our tolerance.

Stephen is dogged, first of all, by his mistake in marriage. He has a drunken wife who constantly leaves

him and is unfaithful to him. He tries to build up a new
life with Rachael but the wife returns. At work, too, he
is at a loss; he is at odds with his fellow-workers and
with his boss.

Stephen can be his own worst enemy; he is an ill judge
of character and confides in people who obviously
despise him, like Bounderby. He is an easy dupe for the
scheming Tom Gradgrind. He is not a man of this
world. He even botches the attempt to clear his name
by falling down a disused mine. Only Stephen, we are
persuaded to think, would choose to travel at night
across a place full of pits!

MINOR CHARACTERS

RACHAEL   Like Sissy, Rachael is a marvellous example of a good
woman. She provides for Stephen Blackpool much
the same kind of support that Sissy offers to the
people in her world. The two women meet only
towards the end of the book. In her anxiety about
Rachael, Sissy asks if she can visit her. Rachael gives
her the highest praise possible for her kind of
influence: 'If it hadn't been mercifully brought about,
that I was to have you to speak to, times are when I
think my mind would not have kept right. But I get
hope and strength through you.'

This is the very same service that Rachael had
performed for Stephen in his trials. Stephen, estranged
from his wife, had fallen in love with Rachael. The
moral pressures of the time made that relationship
difficult – Rachael's good name is threatened by her
being seen in the company of a married man – but she
offers Stephen a sincere and lasting friendship. Her
moral courage is displayed in her kindness, too, to
Stephen's drunken wife. And she continues to look after

her, long after Stephen is dead. Rachael cannot think evil of anyone. She parallels Sissy in the sub-plot.

In her final trial, when suspicions about Stephen's guilt seem confirmed by his failure to return to Coketown, she does find it difficult to forgive Louisa for her supposed complicity with Tom. But later she begs to be forgiven for such thoughts as, 'It goes against me to mistrust anyone'. The real depths of the love she has for Stephen are never made clear to the reader until that terrible moment when she realises that he has fallen into the pit. We then witness a hysteria that could perhaps never have been anticipated in a woman with such self-control. However, it is the emotional expression of one who has, in Stephen's interests, restrained herself for so long. Many a Victorian heart at that point would, no doubt, have wished that it had been possible for Rachael to have made her feelings so eloquently known to Stephen long before the tragedy.

BITZER

Bitzer first appears in the schoolroom but then keeps popping up at various intervals. Thus, we find him assisting Mrs Sparsit, and later involved in the attempted arrest of Tom Gradgrind. His character never develops. He is unfeeling and unimaginative from the beginning to the end.

MRS SPARSIT

Through Mrs Sparsit, Dickens makes one of the novel's attacks on English class-consciousness. Bounderby's claim to greatness is that he has a housekeeper who was related to a good family. She has nothing else to recommend her except this tenuous link with the allegedly genteel Scadgers and Powler families. But such a link, or claim to a link, is enough to establish her worth in the world of the *nouveau riche*. Dickens shows that such a valuation is misplaced, and that she can represent insinuating evil more perhaps than any other person in the novel.

The picture of this elderly widow whose harshness and meanness of nature seem summed up in the mittens she wears, is one of Dickens's studies in repulsion. She speaks hypocritically with 'an affectation of humility'. She is a fitting companion for Bounderby, the 'Bully of humility', for whom she harbours feelings.

Her severe appearance, with hooked nose and 'dense black eye-brows', expresses her bitter moral outlook. She widens the rift between Bounderby and Louisa, and, in her frenetic zeal to re-establish her position in Bounderby's household, hunts Louisa. And she also hunts down Bounderby's mother, Mrs Pegler.

There is some threat of caricature (see Literary Terms) in the depiction of Mrs Sparsit, but this is offset by her many functions in the novel. There is even a point when, after her first meeting with James Harthouse, Dickens seems to suggest that she has developed in that short while some feelings for him; she is visibly disturbed after he has gone.

JAMES HARTHOUSE

James is a stranger to Coketown who is trying to make connections to improve his prospects in life. He is painted as someone whom we cannot trust, who is prepared to use people. He falls in love with Louisa and is prepared to have an adulterous liaison with her. But Sissy Jupe persuades him to leave Coketown.

James Harthouse appears unmoved no matter what situation he finds himself in, and handles people coolly. This gives him a certain attractiveness, yet he has no depth of feeling for anybody. He has always been 'weary of everything' and suffered 'varieties of boredom'.

Mrs Pegler   Mrs Pegler is Bounderby's mother and visits Coketown at different times simply to get a glimpse of her son. He, on his part, has long since disowned her, and has spent his life saying very nasty things about her and his upbringing. Her major function is to help add a sense of mystery.

Mrs Gradgrind Mrs Gradgrind lives in the shadow of her husband. 'Lives' might be too strong a word because she is extremely feeble physically and is never seen in any healthy state! However, she does eventually show some strength of purpose in encouraging her daughter, Louisa, to react against the limited education of the feelings that she has received from her father.

LANGUAGE & STYLE

The opening paragraphs provide many instances of one

Note how Dickens significant feature of Dickens's style: his love of

loves repeating repetition. He likes, for example, to sample single

himself. words: the word 'Fact' is singled out and reintroduced over and over again.

He is fond, too, of the use of repetition for rhetorical effect, and this is exemplified in the reiteration of the same opening of sentences in paragraph two of the novel: 'The emphasis was'. This is not a subtle stylistic device, but its insistent obviousness accords well with the squareness and bluntness of Gradgrind's appearance as described in the opening scene.

Dickens likes to introduce any striking details very quickly. Thus Gradgrind is square, Bitzer light, Bounderby round. These features, once introduced, are there for good. Indeed, Dickens takes obvious delight in ringing the changes on such features by piling detail on similar detail:

*Notice how
Dickens has
obviously listened
carefully to the
pompous way
some people talk.*

Thomas Gradgrind, sir. A man of realities. A man of
fact and calculations. A man who proceeds upon the
principle that two and two are four, and nothing over,
and who is not to be talked into allowing for anything
over. Thomas Gradgrind, sir – peremptorily Thomas –
Thomas Gradgrind ('Murdering the Innocents').

Dickens employs this stylistic trick not in descriptions
of people alone. Detail on detail is the device he uses,
for example, in his depiction of Coketown:

It was a town of red brick, or of brick that would
have been red if the smoke and ashes had allowed it;
but, as matters stood it was a town of unnatural red
and black like the painted face of a savage. It was a
town of machinery and tall chimneys, out of which
interminable serpents of smoke trailed themselves for
ever and ever ('The Key-note').

*Note how
significant irony
is in Dickens's
repertoire of
techniques.*

The grim reality of the town is treated ironically (see
Literary Terms). That end-phrase 'for ever and ever' has
a fairy-tale ring to it; almost as if he were describing
gleaming fairy palaces. Such irony is a further device in
his repertoire. It may take the form of ironic
coincidence as evidenced, say, in the fact that Stephen
and Mrs Pegler – both 'watchers' outside the bank –
come to be charged as accomplices. Or it may be the
grim irony shown in Tom Gradgrind's eventual
dressing-up as a clown in the final scenes, in complete
contradiction of the principles his father had instilled in
him. Or it may be the total irony of Bounderby's
eventual disgrace, through the revelation of the truth
about his mother and his childhood.

Irony is not the only evidence of Dickensian humour,
even in *Hard Times*. The novel may lack that sense of
boisterous good humour that is a feature of many of his
books, but simple humour for its own sake is still to be
found, for example, in his descriptions of people. Thus,
his accounts of the various stages of baldness in

Dickens has a great sense of fun and a great sense of the ridiculous.

Gradgrind and Bounderby show the author in full employment of his own inventiveness. First Gradgrind: 'the speaker's hair which bristled on the skirts of his bald head, a plantation of firs to keep the wind from its shining surface, all covered with knobs, like the crust of a plum pie' ('The One Thing Needful'). Then Bounderby: 'he had not much hair. One might have fancied he had talked it off; and that what was left, all standing up in disorder, was in that condition from being blown about by his windy boastfulness' ('Mr Bounderby').

These descriptions illustrate Dickens's sense of the ridiculous, another example being his description of Mrs Sparsit's relation, Lady Scadgers – 'an immensely fat old woman with an inordinate appetite for butcher's meat, and a mysterious leg which had now refused to get out of bed for fourteen years' ('Mrs Sparsit').

Dickens is not, however, simply pleased to entertain himself. Occasionally, he likes to show someone else gaining enjoyment out of such a facetious approach to life. James Harthouse is used to poking fun at other people, for example, when Mrs Sparsit attempts to be philosophical: 'We live in a singular world, sir', Harthouse replies: 'I have had the honour, by a coincidence of which I am not proud, to have made a remark, similar in effect, though not so epigrammatically expressed.' The tone is effective in levelling mockery at Mrs Sparsit, an effect which is lost on her but can be enjoyed by the reader.

Mrs Sparsit caught in a shower of rain best exemplifies herself as a figure of fun: 'Wet through and through: with her feet squelching and squashing in her shoes wherever she moved; with a rash of rain upon her classical visage; with a bonnet like an over-ripe fig; with all her clothes spoiled; with damp impressions of every button, string, and hook-and-eye she wore, printed off upon her high-connected back; with a stagnant verdure on her general exterior, such as accumulates on an old park fence in a mouldy lane' ('Lower and Lower').

It may be that Dickens's humour becomes rather 'caustic', a word used by Harthouse to describe Tom Gradgrind. Dickens's description of members of Parliament as 'the national dustmen' could stand as a further simple example. It can be seen as poking fun rather cruelly, but it is more fruitful to see it as evidence of his wish to show a childlike innocence and sincerity that are too often lacking in other people in the novel.

PART FOUR

STUDY SKILLS

HOW TO USE QUOTATIONS

One of the secrets of success in writing essays is the way you use quotations. There are five basic principles:

- Put inverted commas at the beginning and end of the quotation
- Write the quotation exactly as it appears in the original
- Do not use a quotation that repeats what you have just written
- Use the quotation so that it fits into your sentence
- Keep the quotation as short as possible

Quotations should be used to develop the line of thought in your essays. Your comment should not duplicate what is in the quotation. For example:

> Dickens says Coketown is a town full of factories and their chimneys: 'It was a town of machinery and tall chimneys'.

Far more effective is to write:

> Dickens paints a grim picture of Coketown as 'a town of machinery and tall chimneys'.

The most sophisticated way of using the writer's words is to embed them into your sentence:

> Dickens is fond of comparing the factory environment with some kind of jungle where the machines are like elephants 'in a state of melancholy madness'.

When you use quotations in this way, you are demonstrating the ability to use text as evidence to support your ideas – not simply including words from the original to prove you have read it.

Everyone writes differently. Work through the suggestions given here and adapt the advice to suit your own style and interests. This will improve your essay-writing skills and allow your personal voice to emerge.

The following points indicate in ascending order the skills of essay writing:

- Picking out one or two facts about the story and adding the odd detail
- Writing about the text by retelling the story
- Retelling the story and adding a quotation here and there
- Organising an answer which explains what is happening in the text and giving quotations to support what you write

- Writing in such a way as to show that you have thought about the intentions of the writer of the text and that you understand the techniques used
- Writing at some length, giving your viewpoint on the text and commenting by picking out details to support your views
- Looking at the text as a work of art, demonstrating clear critical judgement and explaining to the reader of your essay how the enjoyment of the text is assisted by literary devices, linguistic effects and psychological insights; showing how the text relates to the time when it was written

The dotted line above represents the division between lower- and higher-level grades. Higher-level performance begins when you start to consider your reponse as a reader of the text. The highest level is reached when you offer an enthusiastic personal response and show how this piece of literature is a product of its time.

Coursework essay

Set aside an hour or so at the start of your work to plan what you have to do.

- List all the points you feel are needed to cover the task. Collect page references of information and quotations that will support what you have to say. A helpful tool is the highlighter pen: this saves painstaking copying and enables you to target precisely what you want to use.
- Focus on what you consider to be the main points of the essay. Try to sum up your argument in a single sentence, which could be the closing sentence of your essay. Depending on the essay title, it could be a statement about a character: Louisa, finally, is presented as someone who is deprived of love. Saddened by a loveless childhood, she is never to experience the love of children of her own; an opinion about a setting: The bare walls of the M'Choakumchild classroom sum up the colourless world that the children experience; or a judgement on a theme: a central theme in *Hard Times* is certainly that of the hardships of industrialisation. Surrounded as everyone is by the smoke and noise of factories all the characters' lives are touched by it.
- Make a short essay plan. Use the first paragraph to introduce the argument you wish to make. In the following paragraphs develop this argument with details, examples and other possible points of view. Sum up your argument in the last paragraph. Check you have answered the question.
- Write the essay, remembering all the time the central point you are making.
- On completion, go back over what you have written to eliminate careless errors and improve expression. Read it aloud to yourself, or, if you are feeling more confident, to a relative or friend.

If you can, try to type your essay, using a word processor. This will allow you to correct and improve your writing without spoiling its appearance.

Examination essay

The essay written in an examination often carries more marks than the coursework essay even though it is written under considerable time pressure.

In the revision period build up notes on various aspects of the text you are using. Fortunately, in acquiring this set of York Notes on *Hard Times*, you have made a prudent beginning! York Notes are set out to give you vital information and help you to construct your personal overview of the text.

Make notes with appropriate quotations about the key issues of the set text. Go into the examination knowing your text and having a clear set of opinions about it.

In the examination

In most English Literature examinations, you can take in copies of your set books. This is an enormous advantage although it may lull you into a false sense of security. Beware! There is simply not enough time in an examination to read the book from scratch.

- Read the question paper carefully and remind yourself what you have to do
- Look at the questions on your set texts to select the one that most interests you and mentally work out the points you wish to stress.
- Remind yourself of the time available and how you are going to use it
- Briefly map out a short plan in note form that will keep your writing on track and illustrate the key argument you want to make
- Then set about writing it
- When you have finished, check through to eliminate errors

To summarise,
these are the
keys to success

- **Know the text**
- **Have a clear understanding of and opinions on the storyline, characters, setting, themes and writer's concerns**
- **Select the right material**
- **Plan and write a clear response, continually bearing the question in mind**

SAMPLE ESSAY PLAN

A typical essay question on *Hard Times* is followed by a sample essay plan in note form. This does not present the only answer to the question, merely one answer. Do not be afraid to include your own ideas, and leave out some of those in the sample! Remember that quotations are essential to prove and illustrate the points you make.

'The evils which Dickens attacks he caricatures grossly, and with little humour.' To what extent do you think this comment is true?

Introduction

In answering a question like this it is wise to break the sentence down into significant parts. So you would look at what (i) the evils are (ii) what you understand by the word 'caricatures', and whether you agree that it is all done 'grossly and with little humour'.

Part 1

The evil of the education system is one that Dickens focuses on a great deal – it is shown through the physical description and manner of Gradgrind, through the choice of name M'Choakumchild, through the insistence on lack of imagination in school and life.

Part 2

The evil of the environment is seen in the depiction of Coketown with its awful pollution: 'serpents of smoke', 'a town of unnatural red and black', 'the river that ran purple with ill-smelling dye'. Note how often these and similar effects are repeated in the novel.

Part 3   The evil of injustice – contrast between Bounderby's
                  situation and that of Stephen Blackpool – the former
                  well-fed and rich, living in luxury, the latter
                  impoverished and with no escape from a drunken wife
                  and squalid surroundings. No law to help Stephen
                  either at home or at work.

Part 4   Caricature = exaggeration. This can be found in
                  Dickens's drawing of characters like Bounderby as
                  'inflated like a balloon' or as a 'Bully of humility'.
                  Dickens's caricature is often done by repetition of effects
                  in talking about places and people: Coketown is always
                  ugly, for Stephen Blackpool life is always 'a muddle',
                  Sissy Jupe is inevitably sweet and good-natured.

Part 5   'Grossly and with little humour' suggests that there is
                  little use of contrast in the book. Important to show
                  that there is humour in evidence: the circus people are
                  affectionately described – the description of
                  Bounderby's and Gradgrind's baldness shows Dickens
                  enjoying himself; the scene in Chapter 16 of Book the
                  First where Bounderby has to tell Mrs Sparsit that he is
                  going to marry Louisa (he has the smelling salts
                  ready!); the scene in Chapter 5 of Book the Third
                  where Bounderby's mother is revealed much to the
                  embarrassment of Mrs Sparsit.

Conclusion   Dickens does concentrate a lot on the ugly and the gross
                  in *Hard Times*. It is basically an unhappy study of the
                  evils that surround people as a result of industrialisation
                  and injustice. But the artist offers variety and balance
                  through the lighter effects of humour.

Outline a plan as above and attempt to answer the following questions.

1 What is the part played by Sissy Jupe in *Hard Times*?

2 'The plot moves along at a cracking pace.' Show how this is true of *Hard Times*.

3 Show how Gradgrind's point of view about education changes during the course of this novel.

4 Examine one episode where Dickens's skill with language particularly impressed you.

5 Examine the character of Stephen Blackpool and his part in the novel.

6 'Dickens seems fascinated in *Hard Times* by the subject of marriage and family life.' Show how true this is from your reading of the novel.

7 Which event in the novel did you find most sad? Give reasons for your answer.

8 Remind yourself of the scene where Louisa confronts her father and accuses him of spoiling her life (Book the First, Chapter 12). What were Louisa's particular complaints on that occasion and what do we learn of Gradgrind from his reaction?

9 'There is a great deal of humour in *Hard Times*.' What have you found amusing in characters and in incidents in the novel?

10 Who in the novel do you think had the hardest time? Give reasons for your answer.

11 Examine the part played in *Hard Times* by Mrs Sparsit, James Harthouse and Bitzer.

12 'Money and a lack of money are of great importance in the novel.' How true have you found that statement to be?

CULTURAL CONNECTIONS

BROADER PERSPECTIVES

There are several videos that would prove useful to you in the study of *Hard Times*. For example, you can obtain a video called *Dickens of London* published by Yorkshire International Multimedia Ltd, TV Centre, Leeds LS3 1JS (reference number YD 1833).

Two dramatised versions of *Hard Times* are available from: Trumedia, P.O. Box 374, Headington OX3 7NT. Both are BBC productions. Alternatively, there is an audio, abridged reading by Penguin Audiobooks.

There are, too, some attractive books available from libraries. Angus Wilson's *The World of Charles Dickens* (Secker and Warburg, 1970) provides some very readable background material on Dickens. John Butt and Kathleen Tillotson's *Dickens at Home* (Methuen, 1957) gives us some insight into how Dickens produced the serialised version of *Hard Times*.

Another fascinating book is Philip Collins's *Dickens, The Critical Heritage* (Routledge & Kegan Paul, 1971). Here you can read a variety of opinions on *Hard Times* expressed over the years.

You may also like to look at some more recent books on Dickens, in particular Peter Ackroyd's *Introduction to Charles Dickens* (Sinclair-Stevenson, 1991) and A.E. Dyson's *Dickens* (Sussex Publications, 1982). Norman Page has written a book specifically on this novel: *Dickens's Hard Times* (Macmillan, 1979), and you will probably also find Keith Selby's *How to Read a Charles Dickens Novel* (Macmillan, 1989) useful.

LITERARY TERMS

allegory a situation or story which has two meanings, one literal, one deeper or hidden

caricature a grotesque, one-sided exaggeration of certain personality traits, at the expense of a rounded interpretation of character

epitomise to express or represent strikingly an entire class or type; to be an embodiment of something

imagery the use of comparisons or vivid word-pictures to produce mental images

irony saying one thing while meaning another, in order to achieve meaning by understatement, concealment or allusion

stereotype a fixed, standard idea or stock character

symbol a material object used to represent something invisible like an idea or quality

TEST ANSWERS

TEST YOURSELF (Book the First: Sowing)

A
1 Gradgrind *(Chapter 1)*
2 Louisa *(Chapter 4)*
3 Stephen *(Chapter 10)*
4 Bounderby *(Chapter 11)*
5 Signor Jupe *(Chapter 6)*
6 Stephen's wife *(Chapter 11)*

TEST YOURSELF (Book the Second: Reaping)

A
1 Bitzer *(Chapter 1)*
2 Slackbridge *(Chapter 4)*
3 Mrs Gradgrind *(Chapter 9)*
4 Louisa *(Chapter 12)*
5 Bitzer *(Chapter 1)*
6 Tom *(Chapter 1)*

TEST YOURSELF (Book the Third: Garnering)

A
1 Gradgrind *(Chapter 1)*
2 Harthouse *(Chapter 2)*
3 Mrs Pegler *(Chapter 5)*
4 Tom *(Chapter 7)*
5 Louisa *(Chapter 1)*
6 Mrs Sparsit *(Chapter 9)*

NOTES

NOTES

NOTES

NOTES

GCSE and equivalent levels (£3.50 each)

Maya Angelou
I Know Why the Caged Bird Sings

Jane Austen
Pride and Prejudice

Harold Brighouse
Hobson's Choice

Charlotte Brontë
Jane Eyre

Emily Brontë
Wuthering Heights

Charles Dickens
David Copperfield

Charles Dickens
Great Expectations

Charles Dickens
Hard Times

George Eliot
Silas Marner

William Golding
Lord of the Flies

Willis Hall
The Long and the Short and the Tall

Thomas Hardy
Far from the Madding Crowd

Thomas Hardy
The Mayor of Casterbridge

Thomas Hardy
Tess of the d'Urbervilles

L.P. Hartley
The Go-Between

Seamus Heaney
Selected Poems

Susan Hill
I'm the King of the Castle

Barry Hines
A Kestrel for a Knave

Louise Lawrence
Children of the Dust

Harper Lee
To Kill a Mockingbird

Laurie Lee
Cider with Rosie

Arthur Miller
A View from the Bridge

Arthur Miller
The Crucible

Robert O'Brien
Z for Zachariah

George Orwell
Animal Farm

J.B. Priestley
An Inspector Calls

Willy Russell
Educating Rita

Willy Russell
Our Day Out

J.D. Salinger
The Catcher in the Rye

William Shakespeare
Henry V

William Shakespeare
Julius Caesar

William Shakespeare
Macbeth

William Shakespeare
A Midsummer Night's Dream

William Shakespeare
The Merchant of Venice

William Shakespeare
Romeo and Juliet

William Shakespeare
The Tempest

William Shakespeare
Twelfth Night

George Bernard Shaw
Pygmalion

R.C. Sherriff
Journey's End

Rukshana Smith
Salt on the snow

John Steinbeck
Of Mice and Men

R.L. Stevenson
Dr Jekyll and Mr Hyde

Robert Swindells
Daz 4 Zoe

Mildred D. Taylor
Roll of Thunder, Hear My Cry

Mark Twain
The Adventures of Huckleberry Finn

James Watson
Talking in Whispers

A Choice of Poets

Nineteenth Century Short Stories

Poetry of the First World War

Six Women Poets

Advanced level (£3.99 each)

Margaret Atwood
The Handmaid's Tale

William Blake
Songs of Innocence and of Experience

Emily Brontë
Wuthering Heights

Geoffrey Chaucer
The Wife of Bath's Prologue and Tale

Joseph Conrad
Heart of Darkness

Charles Dickens
Great Expectations

F. Scott Fitzgerald
The Great Gatsby

Thomas Hardy
Tess of the d'Urbervilles

James Joyce
Dubliners

Arthur Miller
Death of a Salesman

William Shakespeare
Antony and Cleopatra

William Shakespeare
Hamlet

William Shakespeare
King Lear

William Shakespeare
The Merchant of Venice

William Shakespeare
Romeo and Juliet

William Shakespeare
The Tempest

Mary Shelley
Frankenstein

Alice Walker
The Color Purple

Tennessee Williams
A Streetcar Named Desire

Jane Austen
Emma

Jane Austen
Pride and Prejudice

Charlotte Brontë
Jane Eyre

Seamus Heaney
Selected Poems

William Shakespeare
Much Ado About Nothing

William Shakespeare
Othello

John Webster
The Duchess of Malfi

Chinua Achebe
Things Fall Apart

Edward Albee
Who's Afraid of Virginia Woolf?

Jane Austen
Mansfield Park

Jane Austen
Northanger Abbey

Jane Austen
Persuasion

Jane Austen
Sense and Sensibility

Samuel Beckett
Waiting for Godot

Alan Bennett
Talking Heads

John Betjeman
Selected Poems

Robert Bolt
A Man for All Seasons

Robert Burns
Selected Poems

Lord Byron
Selected Poems

Geoffrey Chaucer
The Franklin's Tale

Geoffrey Chaucer
The Merchant's Tale

Geoffrey Chaucer
The Miller's Tale

Geoffrey Chaucer
The Nun's Priest's Tale

Geoffrey Chaucer
Prologue to the Canterbury Tales

Samuel Taylor Coleridge
Selected Poems

Daniel Defoe
Moll Flanders

Daniel Defoe
Robinson Crusoe

Shelagh Delaney
A Taste of Honey

Charles Dickens
Bleak House

Charles Dickens
Oliver Twist

Emily Dickinson
Selected Poems

John Donne
Selected Poems

Douglas Dunn
Selected Poems

George Eliot
Middlemarch

George Eliot
The Mill on the Floss

T.S. Eliot
The Waste Land

T.S. Eliot
Selected Poems

Henry Fielding
Joseph Andrews

E.M. Forster
Howards End

E.M. Forster
A Passage to India

John Fowles
The French Lieutenant's Woman

Brian Friel
Translations

Elizabeth Gaskell
North and South

Oliver Goldsmith
She Stoops to Conquer

Graham Greene
Brighton Rock

Thomas Hardy
Jude the Obscure

Thomas Hardy
Selected Poems

Nathaniel Hawthorne
The Scarlet Letter

Ernest Hemingway
The Old Man and the Sea

Homer
The Iliad

Homer
The Odyssey

Aldous Huxley
Brave New World

Ben Jonson
The Alchemist

Ben Jonson
Volpone

James Joyce
A Portrait of the Artist as a Young Man

John Keats
Selected Poems

Philip Larkin
Selected Poems

D.H. Lawrence
The Rainbow

D.H. Lawrence
Sons and Lovers

D.H. Lawrence
Women in Love

Christopher Marlowe
Doctor Faustus

John Milton
Paradise Lost Bks I & II

John Milton
Paradise Lost IV & IX

Sean O'Casey
Juno and the Paycock

George Orwell
Nineteen Eighty-four

John Osborne
Look Back in Anger

Wilfred Owen
Selected Poems

Harold Pinter
The Caretaker

Sylvia Plath
Selected Works

Alexander Pope
Selected Poems

Jean Rhys
Wide Sargasso Sea

William Shakespeare
As You Like It

William Shakespeare
Coriolanus

William Shakespeare
Henry IV Pt 1

William Shakespeare
Henry V

William Shakespeare
Julius Caesar

William Shakespeare
Measure for Measure

William Shakespeare
Much Ado About Nothing

William Shakespeare
A Midsummer Night's Dream

William Shakespeare
Richard II

William Shakespeare
Richard III

William Shakespeare
Sonnets

William Shakespeare
The Taming of the Shrew

William Shakespeare
The Winter's Tale

George Bernard Shaw
Arms and the Man

George Bernard Shaw
Saint Joan

Richard Brinsley Sheridan
The Rivals

Muriel Spark
The Prime of Miss Jean Brodie

John Steinbeck
The Grapes of Wrath

John Steinbeck
The Pearl

Tom Stoppard
*Rosencrantz and Guildenstern
are Dead*

Jonathan Swift
Gulliver's Travels

John Millington Synge
*The Playboy of the Western
World*

W.M. Thackeray
Vanity Fair

Virgil
The Aeneid

Derek Walcott
Selected Poems

Oscar Wilde
*The Importance of Being
Earnest*

Tennessee Williams
Cat on a Hot Tin Roof

Tennessee Williams
The Glass Menagerie

Virginia Woolf
Mrs Dalloway

Virginia Woolf
To the Lighthouse

William Wordsworth
Selected Poems

W.B. Yeats
Selected Poems

York Notes – the Ultimate Literature Guides

York Notes are recognised as the best literature study guides. If you have enjoyed using this book and have found it useful, you can now order others directly from us – simply follow the ordering instructions below.

HOW TO ORDER

Decide which title(s) you require and then order in one of the following ways:

Booksellers
All titles available from good bookstores.

By post
List the title(s) you require in the space provided overleaf, select your method of payment, complete your name and address details and return your completed order form and payment to:
Addison Wesley Longman Ltd
PO BOX 88
Harlow
Essex CM19 5SR

By phone
Call our Customer Information Centre on 01279 623923 to place your order, quoting mail number: HEYN1.

By fax
Complete the order form overleaf, ensuring you fill in your name and address details and method of payment, and fax it to us on 01279 414130.

By e-mail
E-mail your order to us on awlhe.orders@awl.co.uk listing title(s) and quantity required and providing full name and address details as requested overleaf. Please quote mail number: HEYN1. Please do not send credit card details by e-mail.

York Notes Order Form

Titles required:

Quantity	Title/ISBN	Price

Sub total _____

Please add £2.50 postage & packing _____

(*P & P is free for orders over £50*) _____

Total _____

Mail no: HEYN1

Your Name _____

Your Address _____

Postcode _____ Telephone _____

Method of payment

☐ I enclose a cheque or a P/O for £_____ made payable to Addison Wesley Longman Ltd

☐ Please charge my Visa/Access/AMEX/Diners Club card
Number _____ Expiry Date _____
Signature _____ Date _____

(please ensure that the address given above is the same as for your credit card)

Prices and other details are correct at time of going to press but may change without notice. All orders are subject to status.

☐ *Please tick this box if you would like a complete listing of Longman Study Guides (suitable for GCSE and A-level students)*

🌐 York Press

📘 Longman

Addison
Wesley
Longman

y